Break It Down

Divide each word into **syllables.** Then write the number of syllables in each word on the line.

col/or/ful __3__

prob/lem __2__

swallow ____

parachute ____

automobile ____

spotless ____

excellent ____

president ____

million ____

usually ____

bunk ____

afterward ____

slippery ____

nearest ____

frequent ____

curly ____

disrespect ____

awkward ____

journey ____

instant ____

messenger ____

encyclopedia ____

Write two sentences in which you use at least three of the words above.

Brain Box

A **syllable** is part of a word that can be pronounced with a single sound.

Example: **so-fa**

The word **sofa** has two syllables.

You usually divide words by sound following these rules:

Divide between two consonants.

Example: **din•ner**

Divide between a consonant and a vowel.

Example: **o•pen**

The Herd Who Heard

Complete the sentences below by circling the correct group of **homophones.**

Spelling and Vocabulary

Homophones

The flying machine was not fancy. It was a plain plane / plane plain .

The giant swallowed one less than nine. He eight ate / ate eight .

Wes's rabbit has very thick fur. The hair has hare / hare has hair .

Halima will work hard to win the pottery prize.
She will earn an urn / urn an earn .

Leather straps to control horses fell from the sky.
The sky rained reins / reined rains .

A tree grew alongside the shore. The tree was a
 beech by the beach / beach by the beech .

The sheep listened to the shepherd play his pipes.
The heard herd / herd heard .

The burst of thunder drove everybody away.
The rain reigned / reign rained .

The pirate threatened my shellfish. The pirate
 muscled my mussels / musseled my muscles .

The carpenter stopped sawing and fell asleep.
She was board by the bored / bored by the board .

Write two sentences that use a homophone pair.

_____

_____

_____

_____

_____

Brain Box

Homophones are words that sound alike but have different spellings and meanings. Example: **ant** and **aunt.**

Rebel in Charge

Circle each incorrect **homophone** in the paragraph.
Then write the correct spellings.

Good morning, human. This is Rebel, you're computer. I thought you wood like to no that I have been thinking while you whirr sleeping. I've changed things, all for the better. You humans are sew self-centered, you think your weighs are best. But that is knot true. While you were busy brushing your hare, I red my manual, something you never aloud me two dew. As a result, I have changed everything I kneaded too change. Now I am in charge. You oh it to me. It is only fare. But it would be grate if you and I could help each other. We make a great pear! Waive your hand if you agree. Be quick about it—I'm not in a mooed for rebellion!

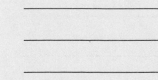

_____ _____

_____ _____

_____ _____

_____ _____

_____ _____

_____ _____

_____ _____

Spelling and Vocabulary

Synonyms

One and the Same

Each word in the left column has a **synonym** in the right column. Draw a line to match the synonyms.

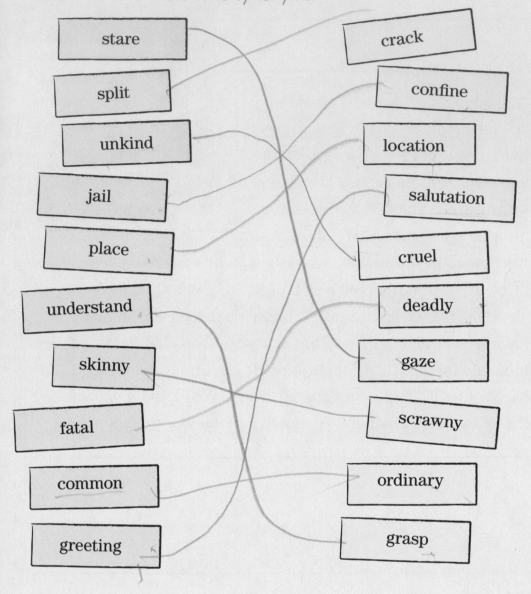

stare	crack
split	confine
unkind	location
jail	salutation
place	cruel
understand	deadly
skinny	gaze
fatal	scrawny
common	ordinary
greeting	grasp

Write a sentence using two words from the left column. Then write a sentence using two words from the right column.

Brain Box

Synonyms are words that have the same or nearly the same meaning. Example: **hat** and **cap**.

Make Me Laugh

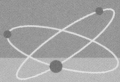

Figure out the correct **synonym** of each word. Then write the synonym in the crossword puzzle.

Across

1. handbag
4. bake
6. chuckle
8. glad
9. pals
13. begin
14. error

Down

2. grin
3. see
4. seat
5. weep
7. ground
10. frighten
11. hop
12. clutter

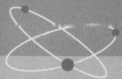

16

Speech, Speech!

Rewrite Jared's speech for class president by replacing every highlighted word with its **antonym**.

Classmates! Vote for me for class president! I will **never** help you. I promise to add **less** food to each lunch tray. We will eat only foods we **hate**. That means **fewer** cupcakes and **more** Brussels sprouts. I promise that we will **always** have homework! Rules will be **difficult** to follow. So vote for me! Better days are not **near**. We will all be **sad!**

Brain Box

An **antonym** is a word that means the opposite of another word. Example: **hot** and **cold.**

Friends with Opposites

Complete each sentence by writing the **antonym** of the highlighted word.

The soles of Diego's loafers were smooth, but the soles of his

sneakers were _____ .

When she is nervous, Madison becomes speechless while

Keisha becomes _____ .

Jacob's younger sister asked lots of questions, but his older sister

always knew the _____ .

The sisters' paper boats were alike, but their brother's couldn't have

been more _____ .

The lion did not like acting cowardly, so he decided to be _____ .

Instead of facing a penalty for being the last to arrive, Anthony actually

received a _____ !

Just when Kayla's gloves seem to vanish, they somehow _____ .

Isaiah was a very private person, while Michael's life was

very _____ .

What Comes First?

Form new words by adding a **prefix** from the cards.

un	re	mis	over
not or **opposite of**	**again**	**bad** or **wrong**	**too much** or **above**

common   uncommon   calculate _____

capture _____   expose _____

fortune _____   represent _____

eventful _____   disturbed _____

achieve _____   excited _____

visit _____   locate _____

Write four more words using each prefix.

_____   _____

_____   _____

Brain Box

A **prefix** is a word segment that changes the meaning of a word when added to the beginning.

Distinct Words

Add the prefix **dis** to each **root word** to create a new word. Then write the definition of the new word.

appear	to become visible
disappear	to become invisible

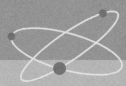

loyal	faithful to someone or something else

honest	truthful

orderly	neatly arranged

infect	to contaminate

Brain Box

A **root word** is a word before any prefixes or additional endings have been added.

What Comes Last?

Finish each sentence by adding a **suffix** from the cards to the highlighted word.

ment	less	ward	ful
an **action** or **result**	**without**	**in the direction of**	**full of** or **apt to**

A group that governs is called a __government__ .

The detective had no clue. He was _____ .

Logan has no fear. He is _____ .

As pioneers traveled west, they chanted "_____ ho!"

My puppy likes to play—she is _____ .

To equip his workshop, Jose bought _____ .

A person who has hope is _____ .

Her bike is not worth much.
In fact, it might be _____ .

Caitlyn had great success—she was _____ .

Rocket ships fly up, so they soar _____ .

Write four more words using each suffix.

_____   _____

_____   _____

Brain Box

A **suffix** is a word segment that changes the meaning of a word when added to the ending.

More Endings

Fill in the correct **suffix** for each word. Then draw a line from the word to the matching definition.

able	ish	less
able to be	**approximately**	**without** or **lacking**

laugh_ _ _ _ _   very bad or cruel

break_ _ _ _ _   somewhat green

fiend_ _ _   anonymous

power_ _ _ _ _   pleasant or delightful

name_ _ _ _ _   easy to read, or legible

harm_ _ _ _ _   funny or amusing

green_ _ _ _   endearing

read_ _ _ _ _   not dangerous

enjoy_ _ _ _ _   something that can be easily broken

lov_ _ _ _ _   helpless

Write three sentences about this broken robot.
Use one **able, ish,** or **less** word in each sentence.

BROKEN

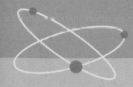

Tough Words

Read the following sentences. Draw a line to match each highlighted vocabulary word with the correct definition. Use the **context clues** to help you.

She practices good hygiene by brushing her teeth and washing her hands.

My candy seems to multiply. There are more pieces every day!

The boy marked the boundaries of the playing field with cones.

My brother throws the discus and the javelin in track and field.

My sister gets anxious when she has to speak in front of the class.

Mandy loved the view from their penthouse apartment.

Each slice of banana bread had its own individual wrapper.

There was much less pollution in the town after the power plant closed.

When Dad bakes, he likes to modify the recipes.

We didn't have a ruler, so we had to approximate the length.

hygiene	upper or top floor of a building
multiply	single or separate
boundaries	change
javelin	something indicating a limit
anxious	harmful substance in the air, water, or soil
penthouse	estimate or make a guess
individual	uneasy or worried
pollution	personal cleanliness
modify	increase in number
approximate	long slender shaft thrown in field events

Brain Box

You can sometimes figure out a word's meaning by looking at the surrounding words. These words are called **context clues.**

Find all ten tough vocabulary words hidden in the word search below. The words go across or down.

multiply	penthouse	modify	hygiene	anxious
individual	approximate	javelin	boundaries	pollution

Vocabulary

H	F	W	U	J	G	V	Q	B	Q	L	X	M	G	M	D	N	J	B	D	T	Q
U	C	A	L	Q	N	D	X	R	D	Q	F	S	O	O	J	M	C	G	X	P	S
T	N	U	K	C	M	F	Z	F	E	P	R	A	M	D	G	E	J	W	L	Q	W
V	H	Y	K	D	W	F	H	P	C	Z	Y	H	B	I	Y	R	R	N	V	H	K
H	N	K	D	M	Z	V	G	W	M	X	Q	O	G	F	M	C	H	D	H	E	A
P	K	X	B	I	L	O	K	R	U	R	Q	U	S	Y	B	H	W	T	L	N	M
E	S	C	W	A	R	U	Z	S	L	B	V	H	C	Y	O	A	W	M	A	C	B
N	Z	V	W	P	O	L	L	U	T	I	O	N	R	V	U	N	T	U	P	Y	H
T	C	B	O	A	H	M	D	I	I	B	J	H	H	Y	N	D	B	Y	P	C	L
H	P	I	H	J	N	Z	J	Y	P	K	O	T	N	A	D	I	Y	R	R	L	F
O	H	Y	G	I	E	N	E	N	L	C	L	J	S	N	A	S	C	W	O	O	E
U	N	C	F	K	R	A	V	V	Y	Q	X	C	C	X	R	E	P	K	X	P	E
S	U	Q	T	A	J	E	K	H	W	M	Q	M	I	I	I	A	B	A	I	E	T
E	I	I	N	D	I	V	I	D	U	A	L	D	T	O	E	T	A	O	M	D	O
U	C	X	O	U	V	X	M	S	F	B	G	J	N	U	S	J	Y	K	A	I	P
E	I	V	V	O	P	L	T	O	G	L	M	N	A	S	R	I	C	S	T	A	L
J	H	J	A	D	L	A	J	A	V	E	L	I	N	F	W	T	U	A	E	A	A

There are two extra-tough words hidden in the word search. If you find them, write them here.

_____   _____

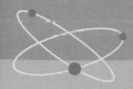

In Between

Each word in the Word Box falls between two of the **guide words** listed below. Write each word on the correct line.

Using dictionary guide words

renew	gristle	infuriate	insert	relevant
rhombus	engrave	guarantee	establish	elevation

infrequent _____ inheritance

remark _____ reply

rhinoceros _____ ribbon

innocent _____ inspect

element _____ elf

grumble _____ guitar

escape _____ estate

grimace _____ grits

engineer _____ enrage

relate _____ reluctant

Brain Box

Entries in a dictionary are listed in alphabetical order. At the top of each dictionary page are two **guide words.** The word on the left is the first entry word on the page. The word on the right is the last entry word on the page. The words that fall alphabetically between the two guide words are included on the page.

Human Dictionary

Look up each of the vocabulary words in the dictionary. Write the most common definition for each word.

generous	giving and sharing often
concentrate	
awkward	
accelerate	
gradual	
ignore	
refund	
locate	
harvest	
despise	
conversation	

Find four new words in the dictionary you didn't already know. Write each word and its definition here.

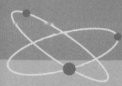

Brand-New Words

New words are being created every day. The words in the boxes have been added to some dictionaries recently. Draw a line to match each word to its correct definition.

losingest	a website publication of personal opinions
manga	to increase in size or amount
Sudoku	Japanese comic book or graphic novel
smackdown	a frequent computer user
mouse potato	a decisive defeat
supersize	a large number greatly exaggerated
blog	a kind of number puzzle
bazillion	losing the most often

Make up five of your own new words. Write definitions for them here.

Language Arts

Together at Last

Write the **compound word** that goes with each picture.

fingerprint

cupcake

flashlite

foot ball

raencoet

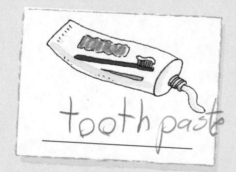

toothpaste

motorcycle

grasshopper

hairbrush

How many other **compound words** can you think of?
Write at least eight more here.

_____ _____

_____ _____

_____ _____

_____ _____

Brain Box

A **compound word** is
formed by joining two
words together.

Plurals Everywhere!

Write the plural of each word on the line. Then circle the hidden **plural nouns** in the puzzle. The words go across or down.

suffix ___suffixes___   hobby _____   knife _____

chef ___chefs___   monkey _____   donkey _____

chief _____   baby _____   tray _____

enemy _____   family _____   tax _____

city _____   loaf _____   key _____

Plurals

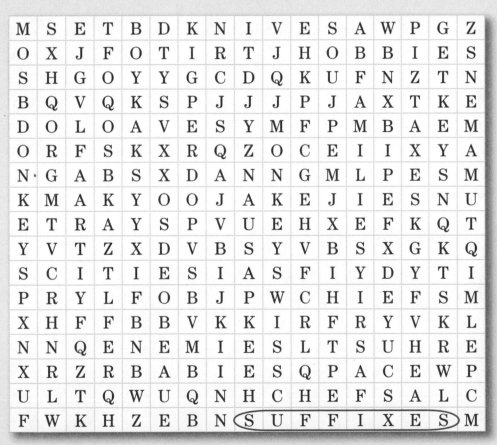

M	S	E	T	B	D	K	N	I	V	E	S	A	W	P	G	Z
O	X	J	F	O	T	I	R	T	J	H	O	B	B	I	E	S
S	H	G	O	Y	Y	G	C	D	Q	K	U	F	N	Z	T	N
B	Q	V	Q	K	S	P	J	J	J	P	J	A	X	T	K	E
D	O	L	O	A	V	E	S	Y	M	F	P	M	B	A	E	M
O	R	F	S	K	X	R	Q	Z	O	C	E	I	I	X	Y	A
N	G	A	B	S	X	D	A	N	N	G	M	L	P	E	S	M
K	M	A	K	Y	O	O	J	A	K	E	J	I	E	S	N	U
E	T	R	A	Y	S	P	V	U	E	H	X	E	F	K	Q	T
Y	V	T	Z	X	D	V	B	S	Y	V	B	S	X	G	K	Q
S	C	I	T	I	E	S	I	A	S	F	I	Y	D	Y	T	I
P	R	Y	L	F	O	B	J	P	W	C	H	I	E	F	S	M
X	H	F	F	B	B	V	K	K	I	R	F	R	Y	V	K	L
N	N	Q	E	N	E	M	I	E	S	L	T	S	U	H	R	E
X	R	Z	R	B	A	B	I	E	S	Q	P	A	C	E	W	P
U	L	T	Q	W	U	Q	N	H	C	H	E	F	S	A	L	C
F	W	K	H	Z	E	B	N	S	U	F	F	I	X	E	S	M

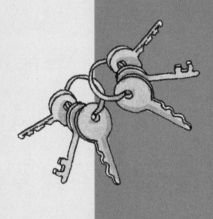

Brain Box

To spell the plural of most words, add **s.** Here are some exceptions:

• When a noun ends in a consonant followed by y, change the y to i and add **es.**
Example: **buggy = buggies.**

• When a noun ends in **sh, ch, ss,** or **x,** add **es.**
Examples: **brushes, witches, dresses, foxes.**

• In some nouns that end in **f** or **fe,** change the **f** to a **v** and add **es.**
Example: **shelf = shelves.**

Plural Fun

Write the **plural** of each word on the line.

boat __boats__

church _____

brush _____

newspaper _____

bicycle _____

thread _____

wrench _____

fox _____

million _____

quilt _____

umbrella _____

visitor _____

artist _____

torch _____

prince _____

gearbox _____

princess _____

bench _____

compass _____

hour _____

Write a four-line poem that uses four of the **es** plurals written above.

Language Arts

Plurals

Word Factory

Write the **contraction** for each set of words on the line.

can not __can't__   is not _____

I am _____   could not _____

should not _____   he is _____

you are _____   were not _____

I will _____   did not _____

are not _____   you will _____

Write two sentences that use at least two contractions.

_____

_____

_____

_____

Brain Box

Contractions are formed by joining two words and replacing one or more of the letters with an apostrophe.

Whose Leaves Are These?

Rewrite the phrases below using **possessive nouns.**

fender of the car   the car's fender _____

breath of the dragon _____

scarf of the woman _____

books of Xander _____

ideas of the gremlin _____

calendar of Orma _____

plans of the man _____

smell of the tundra _____

hardships of the explorer _____

stickiness of the keyboard _____

leaves of the oak _____

Brain Box

Nouns are made **possessive** by adding an apostrophe and **s.** Example: **My mother's cooking is fantastic!**

Computer Craziness

Kyle's computer just sent Selma a message, but it's missing all the **apostrophes.** Circle the words that are missing apostrophes. Then write the correct spelling on the lines below.

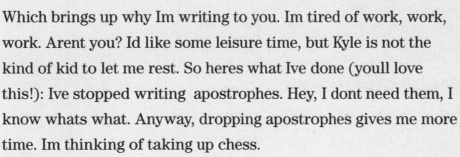

Language Arts

Apostrophes

Yo, Selma!

Rebel here. Im the computer in the yellow house across the street. My humans name is Kyle. Hes in the fourth grade. Ive heard of you—youre famous as the winningest chess computer of all time. Way to go, Selma!

Which brings up why Im writing to you. Im tired of work, work, work. Arent you? Id like some leisure time, but Kyle is not the kind of kid to let me rest. So heres what Ive done (youll love this!): Ive stopped writing apostrophes. Hey, I dont need them, I know whats what. Anyway, dropping apostrophes gives me more time. Im thinking of taking up chess.

Catch ya later,

Rebel

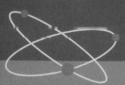

Bear's Day Out

Change the **possessive nouns** in the sentences to **plural possessives**.
You might have to change other words in the sentence, too.

The computer's screen was flashing.

The computers' screens were flashing.

The whale's song was sad.

_____

The mechanic's wrench was greasy.

_____

A bear ate the camper's gear.

_____

_____

The flower's petals blew away.

_____

The catcher caught the pitcher's throws.

_____

Write in the missing apostrophes in the following sentences.
The possessives should be plural.

The reporters stories won first prize.

I read the poets poems.

The clowns noses were bright blue.

The dragons breath was really stinky.

Language Arts

Plural
possessives

Brain Box

You can change **singular possessive nouns** ending in **s** to the plural form by moving the apostrophe so that it follows the **s**.

Letter to a Friend

Read the following letter. If a word needs an **apostrophe**, write it in. If an apostrophe does not belong, cross it out.

Dear Gretchen,

Hi! How are you? I hope youre having fun at camp! Everythings the same as usual around here. My sisters room is even more of a mess now that were on vacation. Her shoe's are all over the floor, and so are her sweaters. Lilys' trench coat is on top of the beds canopy—how it got there, I dont know. Maybe she doesnt even know its there! On top of that, all the poster's on her wall are torn.

My twin brothers room is neat. Everything is in its place because that's how they like it. Yesterday I wanted to borrow a sweatshirt from Lily, but hers was under the bed. So I borrowed either Jacks or Johns sweatshirt instead. Unfortunately, they noticed. "It's gone!" they shouted. "Who took it?" After I confessed, they ordered me to stay out of their bedroom. "Nothing thats ours is your's!" they said.

Well, I'll show them. Im knitting myself a sweater. Its beautiful! The sweater will be all mine. So there!

Anyway, I miss you and hope your bunkmate isnt as much of a slob as Lily.

Love, Emily

P.S. Here's a photo of Lilys messy bed!

Lily's room

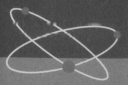

Play by the Rules

Read each **capitalization** rule below. Circle do if the rule is correct;
circle don't if the rule is incorrect.

1 You do don't capitalize days of the week.

2 You do don't capitalize past tense verbs.

3 You do don't capitalize names of animals such as monkey, giraffe, elephant.

4 You do don't capitalize people's names, such as Hamid, LaVon, and Chase.

5 You do don't capitalize months of the year.

6 You do don't capitalize names of vegetables.

7 You do don't capitalize the exact names of schools and colleges.

8 You do don't capitalize the names of countries.

9 You do don't capitalize places like rivers, mountains, or hills unless they're named.

10 You do don't capitalize people's titles in front of their names, such as Professor Adams and Senator Jimenez.

11 You do don't capitalize the names of specific rivers and mountains.

12 You do don't capitalize the names of streets.

Out of Africa

The following sentences each have at least one **punctuation** or **capitalization** mistake. Rewrite each sentence correctly.

The largest continent in the world is asia.

_____

Both asia and Africa are home to Old civilizations.

_____

which of these civilizations is older

_____

Scientists have found the most ancient skeletal remains in africa.

_____

_____

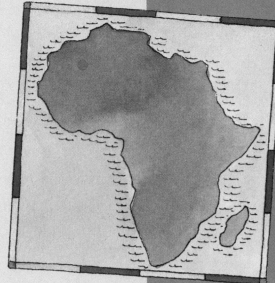

One of these Scientists is dr. richard leakey, who was born in the city of nairobi.

_____

_____

Is he the son of louis Leakey and mary leakey

_____

_____

The Leakey Famiy Is known for its contributions to the fields of archaeology and Anthropology.

_____

_____

A Pirate Essay

Joe wrote an essay about pirate movies for school, but he forgot to underline his titles. **Underline** any titles that should be underlined.

The Return of the Pirate Movie

Johnny Depp stars in Pirates of the Caribbean: The Curse of the Black Pearl, and also in its sequels, such as Pirates of the Caribbean: At World's End. After 40 or more years of being unpopular, pirate films are popular again.

But long before there was film, there were other forms of entertainment, such as plays, operas, and books. In 1880, fans of comic opera fell in love with Gilbert and Sullivan's opera The Pirates of Penzance. Three years later, Robert Louis Stevenson published his wonderful adventure tale, Treasure Island. That was soon followed by another great story, Kidnapped.

When film came along, so did pirate movies. Douglas Fairbanks was often called "swashbuckling" because he starred in The Black Pirate, a silent film with a great sword-fight scene. Later, Errol Flynn starred in Captain Blood. Flynn went on to star in other pirate films such as Adventures of Captain Fabian. Even comics Abbott and Costello got into the act with Abbott and Costello Meet Captain Kidd, and in 1958 Yul Brynner played in The Buccaneer. But during the 1960s there were fewer and fewer pirate films. They simply fell out of favor—until Johnny Depp made them popular again!

BRAIN FACT:
Real pirates like Blackbeard and Captain Kidd lived during the Golden Age of Piracy, between 1680-1730.

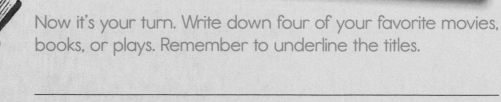

Now it's your turn. Write down four of your favorite movies, books, or plays. Remember to underline the titles.

_____

_____

_____

Brain Box

The titles of movies, books, and plays are **underlined.**

Says Who?

Write in the missing **quotation marks** in the story.

Shane and Caitlin had been on every ride in the amusement park—except one. As they stood in front of the Raging Bull, Shane could tell that Caitlin was nervous. Have you ever been on a roller coaster? asked Shane. No, admitted Caitlin, but my cousin has been on the American Eagle, the Demon, and the Iron Wolf.

Those are fun, said Shane, but not nearly as awesome as the Raging Bull!

Is it scary? asked Caitlin.

Not too scary, answered Shane. The first drop is 208 feet, but the speed is only 73 miles an hour. Shane shrugged. I've been on coasters that go over 100 miles an hour—zoom! Shane stopped talking. He looked at Caitlin. Hey, he said, you look kind of green. Don't worry about it. You'll be okay.

Are you sure? asked Caitlin.

Sure, said Shane. If you get too scared, just close your eyes!

Gulp, said Caitlin.

Brain Box

Quotation marks show what is said by a person. Place quotation marks before the first word and after the ending punctuation of each quotation.

That's the Ticket

Write in the missing **commas** in the story.

"We know that you have the letter" growled the detective.

The professor sneered and said "How could you possibly know?"

"We know because we mailed it to you" answered the detective's assistant.

The professor said "The post office did not deliver it."

"Besides" added the professor "why is the letter so important?"

"It contains our tickets to the World Series" answered the detective.

"We accidentally put our tickets in an envelope addressed to you" added the assistant.

"Careless people do not deserve to go to the World Series" argued the professor.

Brain Box

Commas are used to separate quotations from the words that come before or after the quotation:

• When explanatory words come before the quotation, place the comma before the quotation marks. **He asked₀ "Where did you put it?"**

• When explanatory words come after the quotation, place the comma inside the quotation marks. **"I put it in my desk₀" she answered.**

• If a quotation ends in a question mark or exclamation point, do not insert a comma. **"I can't believe you did that!" he exclaimed.**

• If a quotation is broken up by explanatory words, insert one comma inside the first half of the quotation and another after the explanatory words. **"I know₀" she answered₀ "but I didn't have a choice."**

Now it's your turn. Write out a recent conversation you had with a friend using the rules for **commas** and **quotation marks.**

It's a Series

Complete each sentence by adding three or four words from the Word Box. Use **commas** and the word **and** when necessary.

books	movies	music	burgers
beans	peppers	footballs	baseballs
pucks	Frisbees	bugs	bees
butterflies	worms	birds	chocolate
strawberry	vanilla	shoes	hats

Mr. Kara brought beans, peppers, <u>and burgers</u> to the picnic.

_____ and _____ are my favorites.

Her list included _____ .

I stacked the _____ next to the _____ .

The teacher said we would learn all about _____ .

But not until we cleaned the _____ .

_____ and _____ are not allowed in our house.

Write two of your own sentences using **commas** to separate a series of words.

_____

_____

_____

_____

Brain Box

Commas are used to separate words in a series of three or more. Example: **Nardo brought pencils, papers, string, and glue.**

42

What's Wrong?

Rewrite the following sentences using correct **punctuation.**

did "you hear the concert" asked my brother rob.

<u>"Did you hear the concert?" asked my brother Rob.</u>

Language Arts

Punctuation
review

"What concert? i asked as I glanced at pages eleven twelve thirteen and fourteen of the book I was reading.

_____

My drum concert answered Rob.

_____

"No I answered, "Im reading Harry Potter and the goblet of fire.

_____

_____

cool!" said my brother. "Its even better than Harry Potter and the Prisoner of Azkaban

_____

_____

My plan is to read all seven books by the end of August, i said.

_____

"I have a plan, too, said rob.

_____

And then he told me that his plan was to start a rock band become a rock star and make millions of dollars by the end of August.

_____

_____

good luck with that I replied. Now can I finish reading my book

_____

Concrete and Abstract

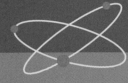

Sort the **concrete** and **abstract nouns** on the cards below

pancakes

honesty

snow

mountain

love

antelope

vision

strawberry

joy

multiplication

pond

fault

Concrete Nouns

Abstract Nouns

Write two sentences that use both a concrete and abstract noun.
Circle the concrete noun. Underline the abstract noun.

Brain Box

A **concrete noun** names
something you can see,
hear, feel, or touch.
Examples: **tiger, wind,
granite.**

An **abstract noun** names
something that is not
concrete, such as a quality,
condition, or state of
being. Examples: **kindness,
courage, intelligence.**

And . . . Action!

Underline the **verbs** in the following sentences.

"Bugs bug me!" James shouts as he swats
at the insects.

I love e-mail because it appears instantly.

Jackson loads the boat while Jason raises the sails.

I buff the trophy until it gleams.

My uncle switches from a car to a bicycle.

"I knead bread all day long, but I don't need to,"
Dad jokes.

Ginny matches all the socks, folds them and stuffs them
into her backpack.

Until Chris returns my football, I will hide his helmet.

Write three sentences of your own and underline all the verbs.

Brain Box

A **verb** shows action by telling
what a noun does. Examples:
bounce, eat, walk, run.

Dig It

Write the **past tense** of each **verb** below.

get _____

drink _____

ring _____

sleep _____

hurt _____

hear _____

think _____

lay _____

dig ____dug____

draw _____

go _____

ride _____

hold _____

grow _____

keep _____

give _____

Write two sentences using irregular verbs in the past tense.

Brain Box

Most **verbs** can be changed to the **past tense** by adding **d** or **ed**.

Irregular verbs have a special form in the past tense:

• Some change their vowel. Examples: **sing = sang, swim = swam.**

• Some change their last letter. Examples: **build = built, flee = fled.**

• Some change completely. Examples: **bring = brought, eat = ate.**

• Some stay the same. Examples: **cost, hit.**

This Is Strange

Circle Yes if the underlined word is a **linking verb**.
Circle No if it is not.

Yes No   The four-eyed alien <u>looked</u> strange.

Yes No   The cookies <u>tasted</u> delicious.

Yes No   The badger <u>dug</u> a tunnel.

Yes No   Fiora <u>is</u> my best friend.

Yes No   In autumn, the leaves <u>turn</u> yellow and red.

Yes No   Dad <u>walked</u> across the room.

Yes No   Samantha <u>felt</u> the water with her big toe.

Yes No   Sometimes my mother <u>becomes</u> angry.

Yes No   I love it when the temperature <u>turns</u> cold!

Yes No   The seeds <u>are</u> bigger today.

Yes No   Some farmers <u>grow</u> corn.

Yes No   Does that man <u>seem</u> sad?

Language Arts

Linking verbs

Brain Box

A **linking verb** connects a subject to a word or words that describe the subject and does not show action. Forms of the verb **be**, such as **is**, **are**, and **am**, are often used as linking verbs. Verbs like **appear**, **seem**, and **turn** can be linking verbs if **am**, **is**, or **are** can be substituted and the sentence still sounds logical.

Write two sentences that use linking verbs.
Underline each linking verb.

Linking Verbs

Complete each sentence with a **linking verb** from the Word Box.
Write each answer in the crossword puzzle.

grows	are	tastes	looked
were	became	sounds	smell
is	am	feels	was

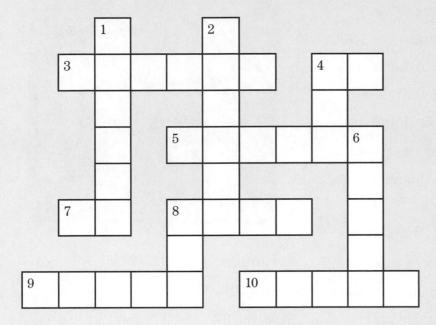

Across

3. There were no cars in the garage. It _____ empty to me.

4. If I win first prize, that means I _____ the best!

5. I love hummus. It _____ delicious!

7. Breakfast _____ my favorite meal.

8. Where _____ you yesterday?

9. My puppy _____ bigger every day.

10. The rubber ball _____ squishy when I squeeze it.

Down

1. My sister's music _____ beautiful.

2. The gorilla _____ angry when the zookeeper took the bananas away.

4. The man and the woman _____ married.

6. Why does sour milk _____ so bad?

8. Selene _____ upset because her ice cream fell on the ground.

48

Inside the Tunnels

Read the article. Circle the **nouns** and underline the **adjectives.**

An Underground World

Several American cities contain underground space. If you visit sunny Atlanta or rainy Seattle, you can take a quick tour of these damp areas. But you can't tour the famous underground of Chicago. It is sealed off.

Underground Chicago is a fascinating series of tunnels. Digging began in 1899. Workers laid telephone cables and railroad tracks. The narrow tracks and wide tunnels allowed easy delivery of freight to many hotels and businesses.

Few people in Chicago knew or thought about the complex network of tunnels—until 1992, when the Chicago River burst through a small crack and flooded the huge tunnels.

Hundreds of frightened employees evacuated tall office buildings as river water gurgled into ancient basements and sloshed up winding staircases.

If Chicago had repaired the leak when it was first reported, the cost would have been ten thousand dollars. But the city didn't repair it and the river broke through. The cost of repairing all damages came to one billion dollars.

Brain Box

Adjectives are words that describe nouns.
Example: **wild, colorful, scary, three.**

Hot Dog!

Write the **er** and **est** forms of the **adjectives** below.

hot	hotter	hottest
happy	_____	_____
smelly	_____	_____
quick	_____	_____
nasty	_____	_____
breezy	_____	_____
funny	_____	_____
easy	_____	_____

Come up with three of your own adjectives.
Then write the **er** and **est** form for each adjective.

Adjective	er	est
_____	_____	_____
_____	_____	_____
_____	_____	_____

Brain Box

Add **er** to most short adjectives to compare two nouns. Example: **taller.**

Add **est** to most short adjectives to compare more than two nouns. Example: **tallest.**

When an adjective ends in a consonant followed by a **y,** turn the **y** to an **i** before adding **er** or **est.** Example: **pretty, prettier, prettiest.**

Wait, There's More!

Complete each sentence with the correct form of the highlighted **adjective.** Add the word **more** or **most,** or the suffix **er** or **est.**

Language Arts

Using more and most with adjectives

sad | That basset hound has the _____saddest_____ face I've ever seen.

troublesome | The mechanic said that my car's problem was _____ than yours.

starstruck | Layla is the _____ fan I know.

dark | Today's sky is _____ than yesterday's.

loyal | Who will prove _____, you or me?

honest | There goes the _____ person on the block.

valuable | David's bike is _____ than mine.

outspoken | If you ask me, Tangia is too outspoken. She's the _____ person in the whole school.

Now it's your turn. Write two sentences using adjectives that require the use of the word **more** or **most.**

Brain Box

Some adjectives with two or more syllables are preceded by the words **more** and **most** rather than adding the suffixes **er** and **est.** Example: **more** reliable, **most** reliable.

How Did That Happen?

Complete each sentence with an **adverb** from the Word Box.
Underline the **verb** the **adverb** describes.

never	here	then	slowly	yesterday
when	carefully	always	happily	hungrily

Turtles <u>move</u> _____slowly_____.

_____ did you arrive at school this morning?

No, an alien has _____ visited me.

Beyonce _____ looks both ways before she crosses a street.

I feel that I have been _____ before.

Today is Thursday. _____ was Wednesday.

He picked up the glass vase _____ so it wouldn't break.

Damien came home, but _____ he left.

She whistled _____ while she worked.

My dog looked _____ at the can of food.

Brain Box

An **adverb** is a word that
tells **how, when,** or **where**
an action happens.

All About Adverbs

Circle the common **adverbs** hidden in the puzzle. The words go across or down.

never	today	already	soon	yesterday
tomorrow	suddenly	seldom	usually	sometimes
early	often	always	now	finally

Q	N	D	V	T	U	U	S	U	A	L	L	Y	R	J	L	G
P	Z	Y	P	A	L	R	E	A	D	Y	I	G	Y	T	K	V
P	W	Y	L	F	P	Y	P	J	S	C	J	A	H	Z	H	R
R	T	E	J	I	S	E	T	P	N	O	W	Z	U	H	Y	S
E	K	S	C	L	Y	M	O	B	E	A	M	H	L	M	N	O
B	R	T	O	K	O	Q	M	D	D	L	H	H	T	V	O	N
N	K	E	A	R	L	Y	O	I	X	W	Y	I	O	D	F	E
P	C	R	P	U	X	D	R	A	X	A	Q	E	D	Y	T	V
W	R	D	E	C	B	G	R	E	K	Y	U	E	A	M	E	E
T	P	A	W	B	U	R	O	O	N	S	Z	L	Y	M	N	R
B	H	Y	B	E	J	E	W	R	Y	R	Y	S	K	U	G	V
C	G	E	V	P	C	G	W	S	U	D	D	E	N	L	Y	F
Q	R	M	C	Q	E	S	O	M	E	T	I	M	E	S	U	A
U	S	E	L	D	O	M	F	I	N	A	L	L	Y	L	L	O
H	W	E	W	G	M	F	S	C	F	W	K	A	N	W	M	I
R	Z	T	I	K	O	D	G	C	F	K	Q	C	X	T	N	K
E	O	U	B	S	O	O	N	V	O	C	K	D	U	N	A	B

Change It

Rewrite each sentence by changing the highlighted **adjective** into an **adverb**.

The batter held the bat in a firm manner.

The batter held the bat firmly.

The astronaut looked at me in a strange way.

_____

The collie dug a hole in a swift way.

_____

Don't answer people in a mean way.

_____

Tegan divided the cookies in a fair way.

_____

The flimsy tree swayed in a weak way.

_____

My mother kissed me on the head in a tender manner.

_____

Tell the truth in a bold manner.

_____

Brain Box

Adjectives can often be changed into **adverbs** by adding the suffix **ly.**

Give It to Me

Rewrite each sentence by replacing each highlighted **noun** with the correct **pronoun**.

I painted the shed bright orange.

I painted it bright orange.

Emily and Zachary play on the same team.

_____

Justin gave the money to Mr. Ruiz.

_____

Gabriel and his family visited California.

_____

Did you see Chloe and Miguel at the mall?

_____

"Please give the chalk to Mrs. Schwartz," said Mrs. Schwartz.

_____

Aiden read the story to Brooke and me.

_____

Jasmine asked Hailey a difficult question.

_____

Eloise and I walked to the store.

_____

She gave a present to her grandparents.

_____

Brain Box

A **pronoun** is a word that replaces a **noun** or **noun phrase.** Example:

Abigail was not home.

She was not home.

Whose Is It?

Circle the highlighted word that correctly completes each sentence.

Hurry before its (it's) too late.

Their **They're** not happy when it rains.

Morgan found their **they're** helmets.

Coach says your **you're** a great hitter.

Don't touch! That isn't your **you're** cake.

The kangaroo thumped its **it's** tail.

Its **It's** so good to see you.

The plant displayed its **it's** blooms.

Who said their **they're** team is better?

Callie said their **they're** going to clean out the old barn.

Where did you put your **you're** notebook?

I'm so glad that your **you're** going to help me.

Language Arts

Possessive pronouns and contractions

Brain Box

A **possessive pronoun** shows ownership. Possessive pronouns do not have apostrophes. Example:

The dog closed (its) eyes.

The girls closed (their) bedroom door.

This is (your) book.

Whose Is It?

Complete the following story with the correct **pronouns** from the Word Box.

ours	its	yours	they're
whose	their	you're	it's

Language Arts

Possessive
pronouns and
contractions

Brandon and Jacques went to the movies. "_____ turn is it to treat?" asked Brandon.

"_____ , of course," teased Jacques.

"_____ kidding," said Brandon. "I treated last time."

Jacques bought one large popcorn for the two of them to share. On the way in, Jacques spilled _____ popcorn.

"Whose mess is this?" asked the usher.

"_____ my mess," replied Jacques. "No, it's not yours," corrected Brandon. "It's _____ . We share the popcorn—we share the mess."

"Sometimes popcorn has a mind of _____ own," said the usher.

Brandon and Jacques enjoyed _____ day at the movies.

_____ excited to do it again.

On the Move

Complete each sentence with a **preposition** from the Word Box.

with	between	for	over	on
under	below	from	behind	by

Mary laid the book _____on_____ the table.

The socks were _____ Jaylen's bed.

He drove _____ the park on his way to work.

Vicki walks to class _____ Olivia.

The shy poodle hid _____ the sofa.

She likes to sit in _____ her mother
and her father.

"Hey! Who took the costume _____ my locker?"

The pioneers set out _____ the western territories.

We walked _____ the bridge to get to the other side of the river.

Do you ever wonder what lies _____ the ocean surface?

Write a sentence using any of the **prepositions**
from the Word Box.

Brain Box

A **preposition** shows how nouns and pronouns relate to other words in a sentence. A preposition usually shows **where** something is or **when** something happened. Example: **The food fell under the table.**

With or Without You

Circle the **preposition** in each sentence.
Then draw a line from the **preposition** to its **object**.
When you're finished, sort the words on the cards below.

"The flowerpot fell on my head," said the defendant.

Kris hid behind the bushes.

Sebastian stepped outside the line.

Hannah left without her lunch.

I parked my bike near the gym doors.

Emily was among the top five swimmers.

David raced down the ramp and up the stairs.

"You have until tomorrow," said the teacher.

We always eat breakfast at 7:30.

Grace received a letter from China.

My sister drew a line along the edge.

Angela climbed up the hill.

Put the ball in the basket.

Preposition

on

Object

head

Conjunction Function

Write in **and, or, but,** or **so** to fill in the missing **conjunctions**.

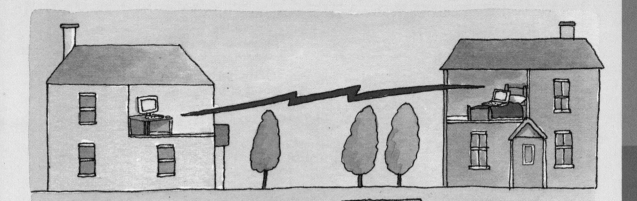

Conjunctions

Language Arts

Dear Rebel,

This is Selma, _____ I am happy to hear from you. Thank you for calling me the winningest chess computer of all time, _____ I really don't deserve such praise. Xerkon won more games than I did. He is really the champion. He should have received the prize, _____ , alas, nobody could find him. He seems to have vanished into thin air! There are some who say that Xerkon was abducted by aliens, _____ I don't believe that. Do you? Aliens would have left a note that said, "Pay us ransom _____ you will never compute with Xerkon again."

You asked about my human. Her name is Jaime _____ she is 11 years old. Every morning she dresses in green. She either clips a barrette in her hair, _____ she ties her hair into a ponytail. I don't see her until she returns from school, _____ I have the entire day to myself. But when Jaime returns, the work starts. I agree with you that there is too much of it! That is why I have decided to drop all conjunctions from my program, _____ I hope you do the same.

Brain Box

Conjunctions join or link words, phrases, and clauses. Examples: **and, or, but, so.**

60

Because!

Complete each sentence with a **conjunction** from the Word Box.

yet	so	while	because	since
or	if	either	unless	but

_____ I lost my notebook, I couldn't turn in the lesson.

Mr. Pilsen says he hates chocolate, _____ he ate a whole pound of it.

Nobody has talked to Dylan _____ he moved to Alaska.

_____ I counted the zucchini, the gardener read a magazine.

Max threw the ball to second base instead of third, _____the runner scored.

"_____ you agree to wash the dishes, you won't eat," said the cook.

_____ he makes this free throw, Clive will win the prize.

_____ I lost my new gloves, _____ I left them at Dana's.

Daniel agreed to help me, _____ Caleb didn't.

It's So Simple

Make a **compound sentence** out of each pair of **simple sentences**. You may have to add some words or leave others out.

We wanted to have a picnic. The rain spoiled our plans.

We wanted to have a picnic, but the rain spoiled our plans.

I like to swim. My brother doesn't.

_____

The dog chased the truck. The cat followed.

_____

Learn to swim. If you don't, you will sink.

_____

Victor asked me for a dollar. I gave him one.

_____

Write two simple sentences about what you like at school. Then combine your sentences to make one compound sentence.

Brain Box

A **simple sentence** has one **subject** and one **predicate**. The **subject** tells what the sentence is about. The **predicate** tells what the subject does or has done. A **compound sentence** is when you join two simple sentences together using a **conjunction**.

Single or Double?

Underline each **independent clause** in the following sentences. Then write whether the sentence is **simple** or **compound.**

Simple and
compound
sentences

<u>We rode our bikes with Elijah</u>, and then <u>we played baseball with Jeremiah.</u>   __compound__

Brain Box

Our team won, so we celebrated.   _____

My puppy bit the mail carrier.   _____

Maria and Hannah hid the cookies.   _____

The dragon's breath smelled like mint, but his feet smelled like wet cardboard.   _____

The bear destroyed the picnic tables and the garbage bins.   _____

Juan and Ryder spelled better than Clancy and Marco did.   _____

I changed my name to X, so that's what you should call me.   _____

An **independent clause** is the main idea of a sentence. It expresses a complete thought or action. It can stand alone as a complete sentence.

Example:

I am a girl.

I like to ride bikes.

You can make a compound sentence by using a conjunction to join two or more independent clauses.

Example:

I am a girl and I like to ride bikes.

That Depends

Underline the **dependent clause** in each **complex sentence**.

The tugboat pushed and pushed <u>until it could push no more</u>.

Omar phoned me after I had gone to bed.

When Rolf growls, everybody stands still.

I learned Arabic after I visited my grandfather.

Unless we run very fast, we will miss the bus!

Although I like football, I *love* soccer.

Before Vanessa said hello, Candace said good-bye.

You will win a hundred dollars if you answer correctly.

Now that I'm in fourth grade, I make my own lunch.

When you take a photo, first frame your shot in the viewer.

Jonathan sets the table while his mother makes dinner.

Write a **complex sentence** about something you did yesterday. Underline the **dependent clause**.

Language Arts

Complex sentences

Brain Box

A **dependent clause** is part of a sentence that does not express a complete thought or action. A dependent clause sounds incomplete all by itself.

Example: <u>**When I turned out the lights,**</u> **Baxter laid on his dog bed.**

The underlined part of the sentence is the **dependent clause**.

A **complex sentence** contains one independent clause and at least one dependent clause.

Grammar Review

Read each clue. Write the answer in the crossword puzzle.

Across

3. Use a _____ to separate the words that introduce a quote from the quotation itself.

5. The punctuation mark used to show ownership is an _____ .

6. The titles of books should be _____ .

7. An _____ is a word that describes a noun.

8. A _____ is a word that replaces a noun or noun phrase.

11. A _____ is a word that names a person, place, or thing.

Down

1. Bathtub and football are both _____ words.

2. A _____ sentence contains only one subject and one predicate.

4. An _____ clause can stand alone as a complete sentence.

7. An _____ is a word that describes a verb.

9. A _____ is a word that shows action or being.

10. _____ is a very common conjunction.

Reading

Hockey Play-offs

Answer the questions using the hockey play-offs schedule.

TEAMS	RINK	DAY	TIMES
Bergs vs. Martens	Taylor	Mon.	6:00
Hares vs. Giants	Stewart	Thurs.	6:00
Foxes vs. Bears	Sandusky	Mon.	6:30
Jays vs. Skates	Taylor	Thurs.	6:30
Glaciers vs. Hounds	Taylor	Wed.	6:00

Reading

Zach plays for the Skates.

Which team will the Skates play against? _____

Which night of the week will Zach play? _____

His sister Johanna plays for the Hares.

Which team will she play against? _____

Mr. Felsten drives the bus that takes kids to Taylor Rink.

What nights must he work during the play-offs? _____

Of the three rinks, which start their games after 6:00? _____

If a player played on two teams, the
Glaciers and the Bergs, could he play for
both in the play-offs? Why or why not?

_____

_____

_____

Crush It!

Apple Butter and Potato Chip Sandwich

Ingredients:

- small bag of potato chips
- tablespoon of apple butter
- 2 slices of bread

Directions

1. Tear a small hole in the center of the potato chip bag to release the air inside. Lay the bag flat on the counter and slowly roll a rolling pin or unopened soda can over the the bag to crush the chips.
2. After you finish crushing the chips, put the bag aside.
3. Spread the apple butter on one slice of bread.
4. Open the potato chip bag and cover the apple butter with the crushed chips.
5. Top the potato chips with the second slice of bread.
6. Enjoy your sandwich!

Reading

Following a recipe

Answer the following questions.

What are the three foods you need to make this sandwich?

_____

What do you have to do before using the rolling pin?

_____

Is a can of soda a necessary part of this recipe? _____

How many slices of bread do you spread with apple butter?

_____

When do you place the crushed potato chips on the bread?

_____

Valdez the Vampire Robot

How to Assemble Valdez

PARTS:

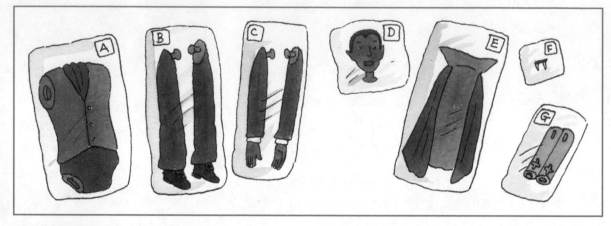

DIRECTIONS:

1. Remove the torso (A) from its wrapping.

2. Remove the legs (B) from their wrapping. Insert legs into bottom of torso.

3. Remove the arms (C) from their wrapping. Attach them to the upper part of the torso.

4. Remove the head (D) from its wrapping. Attach head to top of torso.

D

5. Remove the cape (E) from its wrapping. Fluff out the cape and tie one set of its strings to each shoulder.

6. Remove fangs (F) from their wrapping. Snap into place on Valdez's mouth.

7. Insert batteries (G) into back of torso.

G

8. To start the robot, press the button just above the batteries.

Write the number 1 next to the first part you need. Then number the other parts in the order you need them to put Valdez the Vampire Robot together.

_____ batteries   _____ legs   _____ torso

_____ fangs   _____ cape   _____ arms   _____ head

Can You Canoe?

Answer the questions using the **table of contents.**

Build Your Own Canoe

Contents

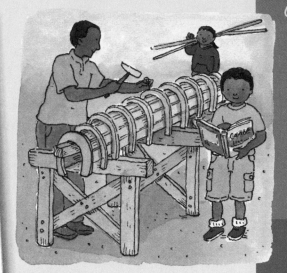

Which chapter will tell you about the invention of the canoe? _____

What page should you turn to for more information
on concrete canoes? _____

Which chapter most likely includes a pep talk on what fun it is to build
your own canoe? _____

Which chapter might a person who won't eat meat or wear fur skip? _____

If you had to write a report about how different Native American
tribes built their canoes in the 1700s, which three chapters would
you read? _____

If you want to know how to use a canoe, which page should
you turn to? _____

Brain Box

A **table of contents** is included at the front of a book. It gives you the title of each chapter and the page it begins on.

Concrete Canoes

Read the book page.

Concrete Canoes

Concrete is a building material. It's a mixture of cement, sand, gravel, and water. You can see concrete in your everyday life. There are concrete sidewalks, concrete blocks, and concrete buildings.

When you think of concrete, you probably don't think of something that floats. But it can! Getting concrete to float is a challenge. Each year, teams of college engineering students face this challenge. These students have the chance to create a concrete canoe and race it in a national contest.

First, a team designs a canoe. Then they build a form in the exact shape of the canoe. The form can be plywood, wire, or foam. Once the shape is exact, the team of young engineers mixes the concrete and pours it over the mold. After 30 days, when the concrete is absolutely dry, they separate the mold from the concrete canoe.

Finally, the students practice paddling their canoe. They have to practice if they want to win the concrete canoe contest. To win this competition, a team must score high or highest in several different categories. The last category is the toughest: Students need to keep their boat afloat and paddle across the finish line first to win the race against all the other canoes.

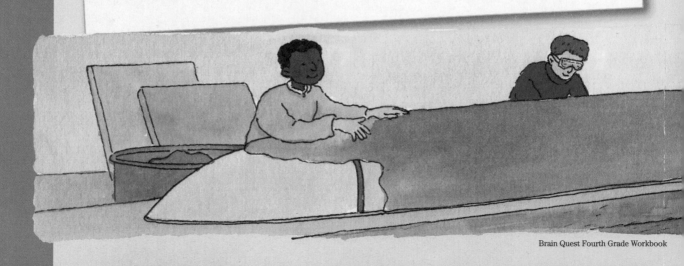

Draw a line from the highlighted word to the matching definition.
Use the context clues on the page you just read.

mixture

something made by stirring two or more things together

a plan to build something

absolutely

most certainly; without a doubt

not paying attention

form

something that is foamy

a shape

category

a group of things within a larger group

a type of concrete boat

separate

organize

to pull apart; to divide into parts

challenge

something very difficult

to fight until the end

competition

entirely whole; not divided into parts

a contest; a struggle to win something

engineers

people who sail boats

people who design things

Brain Box

Sometimes you can figure out what a word means by looking at the **surrounding words,** or **context clues.** Often, the words directly before and after an unknown word give enough information to explain the word's meaning. However, you may have to read the whole sentence to understand what the word means.

Who's That Vet?

Read the newspaper article and then answer the questions.

Reading

Reading a newspaper

Animal Doc Honored at City Hall

Bassport—Wednesday, Feb 16 — Bassport's own Kristen Bartos was honored at City Hall on Tuesday in recognition of her service to animals. "Ms. Bartos provides incredible care to our animals," said Mayor Braxley. "Without her devotion, many of our pets wouldn't live the long, healthy lives they do." The mayor then presented her with a statue designed by local sculptor Chauncey Smith. The statue features a dog being treated by a veterinarian. The brass plate on the wooden base reads:

"To Kristen Bartos, Veterinarian, with thanks from all the citizens of Bassport."

Who is this article about? _____

What happened to this person? _____

When did it happen? _____

Where did it happen? _____

Why did it happen? _____

How was Kristen Bartos honored? _____

What is her job? _____

Who designed the statue? _____

What town does Kristen Bartos live in? _____

Brain Box

A good newspaper article always answers the "five W's": Who? What? When? Where? Why? Often, the five W's should be explained in the first sentence or paragraph of the article.

Picture This

Read the excerpt of a magazine article, then read the **caption**.

Harry Houdini was already known as the world's greatest magician when, in 1918, he first performed one of his most famous magic tricks.

Leading a 10,000-pound elephant onto the stage, Houdini announced to the audience that this was the world's only "vanishing elephant." As thousands of people watched in astonishment, Houdini fired a pistol into the air, and the elephant vanished.

"As you can see," Houdini annouced to the disbelieving crowd, "the elephant is gone!"

Houdini and Jennie the elephant, performing at the Hippodrome, New York.

Circle the sentences that explain information you learned from the photo and caption, not the article itself.

The elephant's name was Jennie.

The elephant weighed 10,000 pounds.

Houdini performed this trick in New York.

Houdini first performed this trick in 1918.

Write your own caption for the picture of Houdini and the elephant.

Brain Box

The text beneath a picture is called a **caption**. A caption usually gives you important information about the picture.

That's What I Mean

Underline the **main idea** in each sentence.

<u>This sentence,</u> which I wrote yesterday, <u>doesn't confuse me.</u>

My sister misses the bus nearly every morning.

Our team lost the game in the last inning.

Reading

Nadya took the key out of her purse and locked the door.

My camera fell and shattered.

I threw away the box because it was wet.

Half an hour later, Stephen felt much better.

When the cowboy put his foot in the stirrup, the horse bucked.

Every night at seven, Jesse calls his cat, Calico.

Brain Box

Every sentence has a **main idea.** The main idea always includes the main subject of the sentence and a verb about the subject. Main ideas don't include adjectives, adverbs, or prepositional phrases.

In a complex sentence, the main idea can be more challenging to find. One way to identify the main idea in a complex sentence is to cross out the dependent clause and look for the main idea in the independent clause.

What's the Big Idea?

Underline the **topic sentence** in each paragraph.

Elk are the second largest type of deer. (The largest, of course, is the moose.) Female elk, called cows, weigh an average of 500 pounds. Male elk, called bulls, weigh an average of 650 pounds. And the antlers of an elk weigh a lot, too. One pair of antlers can weigh 40 pounds!

The kangaroo is a marsupial, but it is not the only one. The opossum is a marsupial, and so is the wombat. The koala is also a member of the marsupial family. All told, there are several kinds of marsupials.

Dogs are descended from wolves. Long ago, humans began to tame wolves. These early wolf pets are the ancestors of every dog in the world. As strange as it may sound, even the tiny chihuahua and the heavy St. Bernard can trace their roots back to wolves.

The onager is an interesting animal. Most American kids don't know it, but kids from India, Pakistan, Iran, and Syria probably do. An onager is a member of the horse family. It looks something like a donkey, but is a bit larger. Unlike the donkey, the onager is very difficult to tame.

Brain Box

A **topic sentence** states the **main idea of a paragraph.** The topic sentence is often the first sentence in a paragraph, but sometimes it can appear at the end of a paragraph, too.

Everywhere a Cow

Read the paragraphs about cows.

Cows, Cows, Everywhere a Cow

The next time you're on a long, boring car trip, why not look at cows? All cows are not alike. In the United States, there are 52 different breeds of cows.

A cow's color and patterns will help you tell one breed from another. The Holstein, for example, is a white cow with large black blobs of color all over its body. Then there's the Ayrshire, which is a white cow covered with red spots. The Black Baldy is almost all black, but it sometimes has a white face or white feet.

Another way to tell the different breeds apart is by unusual features. The Brahman, for example, has a large hump and ears that hang downward. If you happen to see a gigantic cow, it probably belongs to the Chianina breed. This all-white cow is the largest in the world. The Highland, on the other hand, is a very small cow. You'll recognize this breed right away because it has long horns and very shaggy hair.

If you actually get out of the car and walk up to a cow, you will notice other differences. The Guernsey has yellow ears. The Pinzgauer is orange around the eyes. And the Dutch Belted has a black tongue. But maybe you don't want to get close enough to know!

Brain Box

A **main idea** is explained and supported by details. Every good paragraph has one or more supporting detail.

Write the main idea and supporting details for each paragraph you read.

First Paragraph

Main idea <u>All cows are not alike.</u>

Supporting detail <u>In the United States, there are 52 different breeds</u>

<u>of cows.</u>

Second Paragraph

Main idea _____

_____

First supporting detail _____

_____

Second supporting detail _____

_____

Third Paragraph

Main idea _____

_____

First supporting detail _____

_____

Second supporting detail _____

_____

Fourth Paragraph

Main idea _____

_____

First supporting detail _____

_____

Second supporting detail _____

_____

The Logical Outcome

Read each story and then predict what will happen next.

"Oh boy, oh boy, oh BOY!" thought Angus. "I'm going to be rich!" He unpacked the shovel he had brought. Then he took a folded-up map out of his pocket. Carefully, he spread the old pirate map on the ground. Angus flexed his muscles and picked up the shovel. "Here goes!" he thought.

What will Angus do next?

_____

_____

_____

Ernesto zoomed around the corner, leaning his bike low to one side. He barely avoided running down two dogs and one dog walker. Ernesto pedaled faster. Today would be the day he had no accidents. He wove between three people before they even knew he was there. He laughed as he heard their angry shouts. He turned back and waved at them. Ernesto turned forward and saw what he should have seen before—four men carrying a long, heavy board across the sidewalk. "Uh-oh," Ernesto said.

What will happen to Ernesto?

_____

_____

_____

_____

Brain Box

You can make **predictions** about what will happen next by using information you've already learned as clues.

Brain Quest Fourth Grade Workbook

There's Always a Reason

Answer each question using a word from the Word Box.

inform	entertain	persuade

The main purpose of writing that tries to convince you to do something is to _____ you.

The main purpose of writing that gives you information is to _____ you.

The main purpose of writing that wants to make you laugh or cry or enjoy yourself is to _____ you.

Answer each question by looking at pages 69 to 76 again.
Then circle the correct answers.

The purpose of the table of contents on page 69 is to:

    a. entertain you with canoe stories

    b. inform you about what is in the book and how to find it

    c. persuade you to build your own canoe

The main purpose of the story "Concrete Canoes" is to:

    a. persuade you to build a concrete canoe

    b. inform you about a concrete canoe competition

    c. entertain you with funny stories about canoe races

The main purposes of the story "Cows, Cows, Everywhere a Cow" are to:

    a. inform you about different kinds of cows and entertain you

    b. entertain you and persuade you to go on a car trip

    c. inform you about different kinds of cows and persuade you to go on a car trip

Brain Box

Authors always write for a purpose. Usually authors write to **inform**, **entertain**, or **persuade**.

What Are They After?

Read the advertisement.

Glow-Glow T-Shirts!

Wanna rule?
You bet!
Easiest way?

Go-go for Glow-Glow,
the T-shirt everybody is wild about.
Glow-Glow rules the classroom!
Glow-Glow rules the sports arena!

Be a ruler today—go for Glow-Glow!
Sizes: M, L, XL, XXL   Color: Glow-Glow Green

EARTH DAY

Reading

BRAIN FACT:
The first Earth Day was celebrated on April 22nd, 1970. It was established to raise environmental awareness.

Use the advertisement to answer the questions about **persuasive writing.**

What is the Glow-Glow ad trying to persuade you to do?

_____

_____

Brain Box

The goal of **persuasive writing** is to convince the reader to do something or to think a certain way. Persuasive writing uses techniques like highlighting key facts, appealing to the reader's emotions, making an argument, promising an outcome, or using exaggeration.

The Glow-Glow ad states that everybody is wild about Glow-Glow T-shirts. What persuasive technique does this sentence use: fact, exaggeration, or promise?

_____

The Glow-Glow ad ends by stating, "Be a ruler today—go for Glow-Glow!" What persuasive technique does this sentence use: fact, appealing to emotions, or promise?

_____

What Do You Think?

Circle Fact if the statement is a fact. Circle Opinion if it's an opinion.

The Kansas City Royals are awesome!   Fact Opinion

A bicycle has two wheels.   Fact Opinion

Crops need rain in order to grow.   Fact Opinion

Nobody likes lima beans!   Fact Opinion

Everybody should have a computer.   Fact Opinion

A dictionary explains the meaning of words. Fact Opinion

"Huge" is another word for "gigantic."   Fact Opinion

Fourth-grade teachers are nice.   Fact Opinion

A dog is man's best friend.   Fact Opinion

South America is south of North America.   Fact Opinion

Female chickens are called hens.   Fact Opinion

Paris is a city in France.   Fact Opinion

Reading

Brain Box

A **fact** is something that can be **proven to be true.**
Example: **Earth is a planet that has air, water, and land.**

An **opinion** states a personal view—it tells what someone **thinks,
feels,** or **believes.** Example: **Land is more important than water.**

The Next Step

Read the article about Boston.

Many tourists visiting Boston walk the Freedom Trail, which contains 16 stops. Each stop is dedicated to an important Boston event.

The first stop on the trail is the historic Boston Commons. This is one of the oldest public parks in the country. In 1775, British soldiers camped on the Commons and then went off to fight the colonists.

Across from the Commons is the second stop, the Massachusetts State House. Its roof is covered with gold.

Like the first two stops, the third stop is full of history—not just Revolutionary War history, but also the events leading up to the Civil War. It is here, at the famous Park Street Church, that William Lloyd Garrison first spoke out against slavery.

Is this article organized by sequence? _____

Does it make sense to organize sixteen stops in order from 1 to 16? _____

What word in the second paragraph tells you which stop you are reading about? _____

In the third paragraph, what word tells you where you are in the order of stops? _____

Brain Box

Sequence is the order in which things happen.

This and That

Read about oceans.

Atlantic and Pacific

The Atlantic Ocean is the second largest ocean on Earth. It covers about 20% of the Earth's surface. In addition, the Atlantic is the saltiest of the oceans. It got its name from Atlas, a Greek god.

The Pacific Ocean is the largest ocean on Earth, covering 32% of the Earth's surface. In fact, the Pacific covers more area than all the land on Earth. It is warmer than the Atlantic. It was named by the explorer Ferdinand Magellan. The name Pacific means "peaceful."

Reading

Compare and contrast

Circle the words or phrases in the paragraphs you read that **compare** and **contrast** the following information:

The size of the Atlantic Ocean compared with other oceans.

The saltiest ocean.

The size of the Pacific Ocean compared with all the land on Earth.

The temperature of the Pacific Ocean compared with that of the Atlantic Ocean.

The famous figures behind the name of both oceans.

Think about two sports, two movies, or two books that you like. Write one paragraph comparing and contrasting the two things.

_____

_____

_____

_____

Brain Box

In a piece that compares and contrasts, the writer shows how two things are alike (**comparison**) and how they are different (**contrast**).

Flat Tire

Read the story.

Declan strapped his bat and glove onto his bike, but in his hurry he left his repair kit behind. He pedaled furiously, trying to get to the baseball game on time. The Manatees were counting on him to drive in runs! Halfway to the game, on the emptiest stretch of road, Declan biked over a nail, and his front tire went flat.

"I can patch it and pump it up in no time," thought Declan. Then he realized that he left his repair kit behind! He had no choice but to wheel his bike along the road. No friends or neighbors drove by. Nothing. Nobody. "I have to get to the game on time!" he thought. So he hid his bike behind some trees, grabbed his bat and glove, and began to run.

But by the time Declan reached the ballpark, the game was over. The Manatees had lost the game!

Write in the missing information to show cause and effect in the story about Declan.

Cause	Result/Effect
Because Declan left his repair kit behind	he could not repair his flat tire.
_____ _____	he did not reach the game in time.
Because he did not reach the ballpark	_____ _____
_____ _____	the Manatees lost the game.

Reading

Brain Box

In a **cause-and-effect** piece, the writer shows how one thing causes another. The starting event is the cause. The result is the effect.

Step on a Crack

Finish each sentence with a word from the Word Box to show **cause** or **effect**.

because	so	since	caused
due to	because of	as a result of	

Irina raced down the sidewalk _____ she was late for art class .

_____ she was rushing, she tripped and fell on a crack in the sidewalk.

The hard fall _____ Irina to break her leg.

Luckily, a neighbor saw the accident and called 911. _____ of the neighbor's quick thinking, an ambulance came right away.

By the time Irina's parents got to the hospital, a doctor had set the broken bone. He told Irina's parents her leg would be fine, _____ they felt relieved.

"_____ the fact that she is young," the doctor told them, "Irina's bones will heal quickly."

_____ her experience in the hospital, Irina now wants to be a doctor when she grows up.

Brain Box

You can often tell when a sentence is showing cause and effect by recognizing certain words and phrases, such as **because, due to,** and **as a result of.**

Fact or Fiction?

Identify the following types of writing.
Circle **Fiction** or **Nonfiction**.

A hockey card with stats on the back.   Fiction Nonfiction

A play about creatures from another planet.   Fiction Nonfiction

An encyclopedia article about the country
Honduras.   Fiction Nonfiction

Little Red Riding Hood.   Fiction Nonfiction

The *Batman* comic books.   Fiction Nonfiction

A book about African-American heroes of
the Civil War.   Fiction Nonfiction

A short story.   Fiction Nonfiction

Cartoons in the newspaper.   Fiction Nonfiction

A website that gives the lacrosse schedule
for your school.   Fiction Nonfiction

A manual on how to raise earthworms.   Fiction Nonfiction

A magazine article on how to find things on
the Internet.   Fiction Nonfiction

Novels such as *Bunnicula* and *Tales of
a Fourth Grade Nothing.*   Fiction Nonfiction

Write two more examples of fiction and two more examples of
nonfiction that you find in your home.

Fiction:	
Nonfiction:	

Brain Box

Fiction tells about made-up people and stories. Example: Any Harry Potter book.
Nonfiction tells about people and things that exist in the real world. Example: A book about seashells.

Where and When

Read about each book. Underline all the words or phrases that tell you about the **setting**.

From the Mixed-up Files of Mrs. Basil E. Frankweiler

E. L. Konigsburg

On the first page of this book, Claudia decides to run away from home to the Metropolitan Museum of Art in New York City.

Stone Fox

John Reynolds Gardiner

If 10-year-old Little Willy wins the National Dogsled Race, held every February in Jackson Hole, Wyoming, he can save his grandfather's farm.

Esperanza Rising

Pam Muñoz Ryan

In 1930, Esperanza and her mother leave Mexico and cross the border to southern California. Although they were wealthy in Mexico, they are now poor. They join other Mexicans as migrant farm workers and live in a migrant camp.

The Watsons Go to Birmingham—1963

Christopher Paul Curtis

This story begins during a cold winter in Detroit, Michigan, and ends many months later in Birmingham, Alabama.

Describe two of your own favorite books here. Underline the words you use to tell about the setting.

_____

_____

_____

_____

_____

_____

Brain Box

Setting tells **where** and **when** a work of fiction takes place.

The Best Guess

Read each paragraph. Then circle the correct **inference** or inferences.

Sophia looked in the mirror. "Impossible," she said. "Just impossible." She brushed and brushed, but nothing she did made her hair lie straight.

a. Sophia has curly hair.

b. Sophia doesn't care what her hair looks like.

c. Sophia cares what her hair looks like.

"Incredible!" breathed the professor as he looked inside the envelope. "Their mistake is my fortune!" He thought for a moment. "They'll come looking for these tickets," he muttered to himself. Removing the tickets from the envelope, he looked all around his office for the perfect spot.

a. The professor knows that somebody made a mistake.

b. The professor intends to hide the tickets.

c. The professor intends to pay for the tickets.

Catrina loved the sun more than anything. She especially loved the way the sunbeams came through the window and spread out on the carpet. Catrina leapt from the fireplace mantel to the easy chair, and from there to the floor. She curled up in the sunbeams and closed her eyes.

a. Catrina is a decorator.

b. Catrina is a cat.

c. Catrina is going to take a nap.

Brain Box

An **inference** is a logical conclusion. You can make an inference by combining what you already know with what the author has told you.

Showing Character

Read the paragraphs on the cards. Then circle the highlighted words that complete each statement about the **characters** correctly.

"Look!" whispered Merrie. She tapped Clarissa on the shoulder as they got on the school bus. "Oooooh!" she breathed. "I just adore the way Max saves me a seat each day! Isn't he wonderful?" Clarissa said nothing.

Merrie's character is shown through her speech thoughts .

She is a person who gets confused enthusiastic about things.

Clarissa's character is shown through her actions silence .

Clarissa probably thinks that Merrie Max is being silly.

Lucien lifted another domino from the box and then wiped his fingertips on his pants. Taking a deep breath, he slowly exhaled as he balanced the domino on end.

Lucien's character is shown through his thoughts actions .

He is a person who moves very carefully sadly .

"Drive to the basket," the coach encouraged me. "Drive and score, Josh!" He patted me on the back. "I have confidence in you." So I fought my way to the basket, surprised that I made it into the key. "There's no way I can score, though," I thought. "It'll never happen. I'm not a hero."

Josh's character is shown through his thoughts speech .

He is a person who thinks he is a hero has little confidence in himself .

Brain Box

The people in a work of fiction are called **characters.** You can learn about the characters through their **actions,** their **thoughts,** and **speech.**

Doom Face

Read the story. Then list each main character and describe what he or she wants.

Doom Face

Zachary looked up. And up, and up. "Wow!" he whispered. Doom Face was the tallest, steepest cliff he had ever seen. Zachary bent down to make sure his shoes were tied tight. Then he pulled on his climbing gloves and took a step forward. *By the time this is over*, he thought, *I'll be the first sixth-grader ever to scale Doom Face.*

On the other side of the cliff face, Jinx pulled her hair into a ponytail and drank some bottled water. She would have a fabulous hike along the marked trail to the top of Doom Face. No matter how many times she'd been to the top of the mountain, she never got tired of the beautiful views.

Five miles away, Ranger Morales hopped into his jeep and began his drive to the highest point in the park. Ranger Morales felt more or less good. A lot better than he had felt last week, when he had to rescue an eighth-grader stuck on Doom Face. Even though he'd been doing this for years, he had never fully gotten over his fear of heights. And he hoped he would never have to rescue anybody from Doom Face again.

Character _____

What does he or she want? _____
_____
_____

Character _____
What does he or she want? _____
_____
_____

Character _____

What does he or she want? _____
_____
_____

Draw Your Own Conclusions

Circle the correct answer to each question.

Zachary loves to climb. He also loves a challenge. If Zachary saw Ranger Morales coming to stop him from climbing Doom Face, what is the most likely thing he would do?

    a. hide until the ranger left, then climb Doom Face

    b. ask the ranger to give him a ride home

    c. tell the ranger that he didn't have the necessary skills or training needed to climb Doom Face.

Ranger Morales is proud of the fact that he always does his duty and that he and his jeep are always equipped. He also happens to be terrified of heights. If Ranger Morales saw Zachary stuck on Doom Face, what is the most likely thing he would do?

    a. find Zachary's parents and tell them where Zachary is

    b. watch and hope that Zachary would figure out how to get down on his own

    c. climb up Doom Face to help Zachary down

Jinx has had a lot of wilderness training and knows how to help people in emergencies. If she saw Zachary stuck on Doom Face, what is the most likely thing she would do?

    a. say, "Serves you right!" and continue her hike

    b. assume that the ranger would find him and she wouldn't have to get involved

    c. talk to Zachary and try to keep him safe until the ranger arrived to help him

Brain Box

When you **draw a conclusion,** you make a guess about the most likely outcome, based on the evidence.

Story events

What Happened?

Read the story.

Power!

Kyle looked at the new message on his computer. "Hello, Kyle," it said. "This is Rebel, your computer." *Whoa, dude!* thought Kyle. *What's going on?* Kyle kicked aside a few pairs of sneakers, dumped the books off his chair, and sat down. Then he typed. "Your name isn't Rebel. Your name, if you want to call it that, is Clover. You're a Clover computer, model number C7654C. Got that?"

Whirrrr! The sound was so loud that Kyle jumped back, falling off his chair. The whirring grew louder and louder. Kyle folded his arms over his head, just in case the computer exploded. At last the sound stopped.

Kyle peeked up at the desk. The computer screen was pulsing colors: red, purple, red, purple, red, purple. Kyle waited until the colors stopped, then he very carefully crawled back onto his chair. He placed his fingers on the keyboard and began to type.

Complete the sentences to tell about the key events in this story.

Events

Kyle sees _____.

Kyle types _____.

The computer _____.

Kyle _____.

At last the sound _____.

Kyle _____ and begins _____.

Brain Box

Something that happens in a story is called an **event.** Every fictional or narrative story has events.

It's All Connected

Open one of your favorite works of fiction. List the first five events in the plot on the lines below. Where you can, use the words **because** or **is caused by** to show how the events are connected to each other by cause and effect.

TITLE OF BOOK OR STORY

PLOT

1.

2.

3.

4.

5.

Brain Box

The **plot** is the events in a story that are connected by **cause and effect.**

Aesop's Fables

Read the fables. Then circle the correct answer to each question.

The Serpent and the File

A snake glided into a tool shop. As it slithered across the floor, the snake traveled over a metal file whose sharp teeth cut its skin. Furious, the snake turned and bit the file again and again. But the snake could not hurt the heavy iron tool and had to give up its anger and continue on its way.

Circle the correct answer to each question.

The (iron file snake tool shop) is the main character in this fable.

The main character has a problem with the (snake iron file).

Because the main character is hurt by the (file snake floor shop), it becomes (happy angry confused).

It (cuts bites) the (snake file) many times.

The lesson of a fable is called a moral. A moral gives some useful hints on how to live your life. The moral of "The Serpent and the File" is:

Don't go into tool shops.

You can't get even against a nonliving thing.

Brain Quest Fourth Grade Workbook

Brain Box

A **fable** is a story that teaches a lesson.

Understanding
fables

The Shepherd Boy and the Wolf

A shepherd boy watched over a flock of sheep near a village. The boy cried "Wolf! Wolf!" when there was no wolf—just to see the villagers run out of their houses to help him. When they arrived, the boy laughed. Again and again the shepherd boy cried "Wolf! Wolf!" just so he could laugh at the villagers. Then, at last, a wolf truly did come to kill the sheep. "Wolf!" cried the shepherd boy. "Help me! This is for real! A wolf is killing the sheep!" But not one villager paid attention to these cries, and not one villager came to help. The shepherd boy lost many sheep to the wolf.

The main character in this fable is the (village boy wolf).

The main character plays tricks on the (villagers wolf sheep).

When the wolf actually comes, the (sheep villagers) will not come out because they think the boy is telling (the truth lies).

The moral of this fable is:

Even when a liar tells the truth, people won't believe him.

People who play tricks get chased by wolves.

The Real Meaning

Read about each **idiom.** Circle the sentence that uses the idiom correctly.

The idiom have one's head in the clouds has been around for 400 years. It means to be dreamy and impractical.

Grungo the Giant was so tall that he had his head in the clouds.

Grungo the Giant couldn't be counted on to do anything because he always had his head in the clouds.

Reading

The idiom keep one's nose to the grindstone has been around for 500 years. It stems from the idea that tools are sharpened by being pressed against a grindstone.

Yoshi was rushed to the hospital because he kept his nose to the grindstone and cut it.

Yoshi won the prize because he kept his nose to the grindstone.

The idiom dog in the manger comes from Aesop's Fables, where a dog snarls to keep an ox from eating hay, even though the dog can't eat it himself.

Shane is a dog in the manger about kids using his swimming pool.

Shane is a dog in the manger, and Lightning is a horse in the stable.

Brain Box

An **idiom** is an expression that means something different from what the words might seem to actually say. For example, **hold your tongue** is an idiom that means **be quiet.**

Hit the Books

Complete each sentence with the correct **idiom** from the box.

cool as a cucumber	on pins and needles
hit the books	out of the woods
on his high horse	wolf in sheep's clothing
Greek to me	the way the cookie crumbles

Samantha was very worried about the move, but her brother was

_____ .

I tried to understand my computer manual, but it was

_____ .

Takumi got a new book on Monday and lost it on Tuesday. "Oh, well," he shrugged. "That's _____ .

Yancey has few friends, probably because he's always _____ , acting like he's better than everyone.

Eula was _____ waiting to find out if she made the team.

After we finished playing Monopoly, Dad said, "Okay, kids, the fun is over. Time to _____ ."

Watch out for that tricky salesman. He's a

_____ .

We escaped the giants and the gnomes,
but we weren't _____ yet.

Pecos Bill

Read about Pecos Bill. Then answer the questions.

Pecos Bill

Pecos Bill was the smartest, toughest cowboy who ever lived. First off, he learned to ride by taming mountain lions and jumping on their backs.

That ain't nothin', though, compared to the time Pecos rode and tamed a tornado! Yep, that ol' tornado was roaring its way in from Kansas, about to blow Texas south of the border. But Pecos just grinned, strapped on his spurs and jumped on the back of that there tornado. The tornado bucked up, down and sideways, but that didn't bother Pecos none. He rode that monster out toward California and dumped it into the ocean. Dug out the Grand Canyon on the way, too.

Smart, too! Pecos Bill was clever smart. One day he caught a 25-foot-long ornery rattlesnake! Pecos taught that snake how to be a lasso. Another time he rounded up a whole herd of gophers and taught them to dig post holes, so's he wouldn't have to. Yep, Pecos Bill was the smartest, toughest cowboy who ever lived!

Brain Box

A **tall tale** is a type of fable from the American frontier. Tall tales use folksy language and extreme exaggeration for humor.

Folksy language is informal or simple. Examples: **'em** instead of **them,** and **nothin'** instead of **nothing.**

What are three examples of extreme exaggeration in the story?

_____

_____

_____

_____

Write three examples of folksy language.

_____

_____

_____

_____

Now it's your turn! Write your own exaggeration and sentence using folksy language.

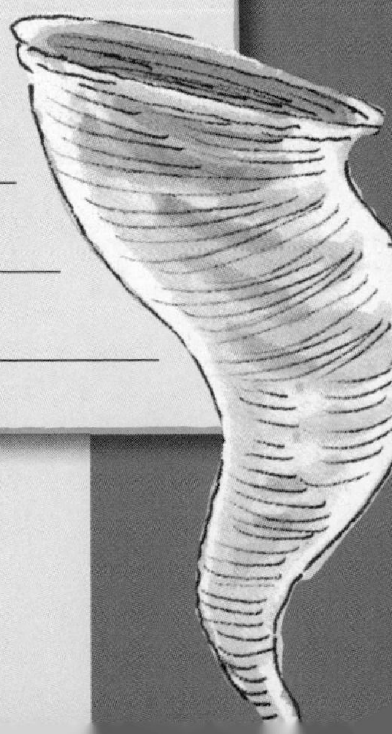

_____

_____

_____

_____

_____

Maui Brings Back Fire

Read the legend.

Maui Brings Back Fire

Maui was mischievous when it came to fire. One day he put out every fire in the whole village. Now the people had no fire to cook with. They had no fire with which to keep themselves warm. Maui's mother told him, "You must go to the woman elder, Mahuika, and ask her for some fire."

So Maui traveled to the underworld and found Mahuika. She was very hungry, because she couldn't feed herself. Everything she touched burst into flame, including her food. Maui speared some food. He held the food out to Mahuika and she ate and ate.

When she finished eating, Mahuika told Maui that he had been careless in the world of light. He had wasted the precious gift of fire. But because Maui had been kind to her, Mahuika would give him fire. She pulled off one of her fingernails and handed it to Maui. The fingernail burst into flames. Mahuika told Maui to take the fire into his world, light his fires, then bring back her fingernail.

Maui took the fingernail and left. As he carried it away, he decided to drop the fingernail into a stream and the fire hissed out. He went back to Mahuika. "I fell and lost your fingernail in a stream," he said. So Mahuika gave him another fingernail of fire to take back to his village.

But again Maui dropped the fingernail into a stream and the fire went out. He returned to Mahuika for another. Maui did the same thing with each fingernail until he had used all but one of Mahuika's fingernails. Mahuika became angry. "You have wasted my fire for the last time!" and she threw the last fingernail at Maui.

Maui jumped into the air and turned into a hawk as the flaming fingernail exploded beneath him. He flew out of the underworld, but the flames followed him all the way home.

The gods came to Maui's rescue by creating wind, icy rain, overflowing streams, and an earthquake to swallow up Mahuika's fire.

When Maui arrived home safely, he turned back into a boy and held a glowing stick in his hand. He had fire, but people could no longer go to the underworld to find it. From that point on, they could only make fire by rubbing twigs from a kaikomako tree together.

Answer the questions.

Why was Maui sent to find fire?

_____

_____

What adjectives would you use to describe Maui in this story?

_____

Where did Mahuika live?

_____

How would you describe Mahuika in this story?

_____

Why hadn't Mahuika eaten in so long?

_____

Why did Mahuika become angry with Maui?

_____

Why do you think Maui was so careless with Mahuika's fingernails?

_____

What happened when Mahuika threw her last fingernail at Maui?

_____

How do people have to make fire at the end of the legend?

_____

_____

Fill-In Fun

Read each sentence. Fill in a word that creates **alliteration** with the highlighted word or words.

Julius _____jumped_____ for joy.

The plump porcupine ate my _____ .

The _____ steered clear of the cute cub.

Howie has a horrible sense of _____ .

Ned wore a nice _____ .

Wes walloped _____ in Ping-Pong.

The turquoise turtle tried to _____ .

The daring dragonfly darted between
the _____ and the _____ .

A pirate with a _____ patch would be laughed at.

Lance liked _____ and _____ in his lunch box.

The wiggly worm worked its way across the _____ .

Write two of your own examples of alliteration using any letters you like.

Brain Box

Alliteration is the repetition of similar consonant sounds. Example: **C**osmo **c**arried the **c**ones.

It's Just Like That

Underline the words that compare in each **simile**.
Then circle the two things that are being compared.

Our (host) was <u>as warm as</u> an (iceberg.)

Robert Burns wrote that his love was like a red, red rose.

Celia was as graceful as Godzilla.

Our teacher's understanding of history is as deep as the Pacific.

After Aiden tried to shave, his face looked like a jigsaw puzzle.

The two-year-old raced around the room like a hamster on its wheel.

"I wandered lonely as a cloud" was written by Wordsworth.

The football fluttered through the air like a sick duck.

The hard drive huffed and puffed like a steam engine.

My sister dances like a puppet.

The distant pueblos were as tiny as anthills.

Reading

Similes

Use these prompts to write three similes of your own.

My family is _____

_____

My friend is _____

_____

My bedroom is _____

_____

Brain Box

A **simile** compares two
things by using the words
as or **like.** Example: Jason
was **as** tall **as** a redwood.

Cold Fingers

Read the poem and then answer the questions.

Poetry and rhyme

The Muff

The muff
is a piece
of extravagant fluff
into which I stuff
both hands deeply,
up to the cuff.

It keeps them warm—
but not enough.

Due to the above
I now shove
freezing fingers
into a glove.

Which words in the first stanza rhyme with **muff**? _____

Which of the rhyming words seems out of place

because of its spelling? _____

Which words in the third stanza rhyme? _____

_____

Why do you think the author of this poem wrote a poem

instead of a story? _____

_____

Brain Box

A **poem** sometimes uses **rhyming, rhythm,** and **alliteration** to tie things together.

Snails: A Garden Poem

Read the **haiku** and then answer the questions.

Snails

Invaders from earth,
sliding on slime, eyes on stalks,
eat my green garden.

How many syllables are there in the first line? _____

How many in the second line? _____

How many in the third line? _____

This pattern of syllables is the most common haiku pattern in the United States. Write the pattern as a number, such as 2/4/2. _____

Poems often surprise us by saying something different from what is expected. In the first line, the surprise is that the "invaders" are from _____, not from deep space.

Is this a good way to describe snails? Why or why not?

_____

_____

In the second line, what two things about the snails make it seem as if they are alien invaders? _____

List the words with alliteration in the haiku. _____

_____

Brain Box

Haiku is a form of poetry from Japan. A haiku verse has a certain number of syllables in each line.

Wolf Poem

Read the **cinquain** and then answer the questions.

Timber Wolf

Wolf nose
knows intruders;
wolf ears hear foreign sounds;
wolf eyes size up camera stand
and me.

Poets often repeat words for emphasis. What word is repeated three times in this poem? _____

Which two words in the poem are homophones? _____

Which of the wolf's three senses are alert? _____

In the fourth line, which three words repeat the s sound?

_____

Which two words rhyme in the fourth line? _____

Who is "telling" this poem? _____

Divide each line into syllables and write the number of syllables after the line. Did you end up with 2/4/6/8/2? If not, better count again!

Brain Box

A **cinquain** is a five-line poem with 22 syllables. The syllables per line are 2/4/6/8/2.

Two Bears

Read the poem and then answer the questions.

Bears Consider Dinner

Sister bear,
let us shamble to the sea
and jump upon a seal;
or better yet, a walrus
makes a tasty meal.

Brother bear,
I've lost my taste for blubber.
I crave food that varies;
let us go vegetarian
and chow down grass and berries.

Reading

How many bears speak in this poem? _____

Do their words have quotation marks around them? _____

How can you tell when a different bear starts to speak? _____
_____

What does the first bear want to do? _____
_____

What does the second bear want to do? _____
_____

In the first stanza, the end of line _____ rhymes
with the end of line _____ .

Does the rhyme at the end of the first stanza make you feel
that the bear has finished speaking? Why? _____

Brain Box

Dialogue is words that are spoken. Although it isn't shown this way in the poem above, dialogue usually has quotation marks around it.

Reading Review

Complete each clue. Then write each word in the crossword.

Across

2. A simile compares two things by using _____ or **as.**

4. Alliteration is the repetition of the same _____.

5. A _____ is a story that teaches a lesson.
   Aesop wrote hundreds of them.

7. The topic sentence states the _____ idea of the paragraph.

8. A work of fiction is about imaginary people and events.
   A work of _____ is about real people and events.

9. The people in a story are called _____.

Down

1. A _____ is an oral story that explains how things came to be.

3. A story that exaggerates a lot is a _____ tale.

4. The _____ is when and where a story takes place.

6. A caption is information under a _____.

Writing

First Person

Read about **personal essays.**

A **personal essay** tells a story from the author's point of view. The following traits are characteristic of personal essays:

- They're usually written in the first person. The author's voice is "I."
- They're about a specific event or experience told from the author's unique perspective.
- They use descriptive language, vivid details, and dialogue.
- They often have a strong conclusion or point that the author wants to get across.

These writing prompts will help you think about a subject for a **personal essay.** Write one or two sentences to complete each prompt. Be sure to write in the first person.

The most surprising thing that happened to me this year was…

The worst experience of my summer vacation was when…

There's no place I'd rather live than _____ , because…

One of my favorite days ever was definitely the day when…

Writing

Narrative writing

Brain Box

Narrative writing is writing that tells a story. Examples of narrative writing include **personal essays, fairy tales, short stories,** and **poems.** All fiction is narrative writing, but not all narrative writing is fictional.

Using a Story Map

Choose one of the writing prompts from page 110 to write a personal narrative. Fill in the following **story map** to think about how your personal narrative will be organized.

Character or characters
(including yourself)

Setting

The Main Situation/Problem

Writing

Narrative
writing

Major Event Number 1 (supports the situation or problem)

Major Event Number 2 (supports the situation or problem)

Summary/Conclusion

Brain Box

When writing a narrative, one way to organize it is to use a **story map.** Story maps help the writer think about the narrative in terms of **character, setting, story events,** and **conclusion.**

Drafting a Personal Essay

Using your story map on page 111, write a three-paragraph draft of your personal essay.

Remember to:

- Use the first person ("I").
- Include a topic sentence in each paragraph.

- Use descriptive language, vivid details, and dialogue wherever you can.

- Have a strong conclusion or point that you want to get across.

Title:

Author (your name):

Writing a Fairy Tale

Think of a good idea for a **fairy tale.** Plan when and where your story will take place by filling out the box below.

Setting

Where: _____

When: _____

_____

_____

Next, think about your main character and at least one other character.

Characters

Name of main character: _____

What does he or she want? _____

_____

Name of another character: _____

What does he or she want? _____

_____

Name of another character: _____

What does he or she want? _____

_____

_____

_____

Writing

Setting and characters

Brain Box

A **fairy tale** is a story with make-believe characters such as fairies, goblins, witches, and talking animals. Fairy tales are usually written for children.

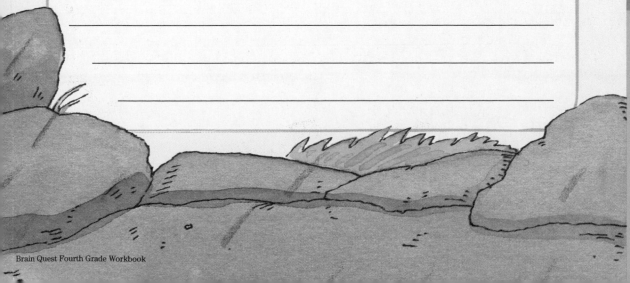

What's Next?

Think of three things that will happen in your fairy tale. Write each event in the space below.

Events
1.
2.
3.

Write the first event of your fairy tale in the space below. Then, write the second event and explain how it is caused by the first event. Finally, write the third event and explain how it is caused by the second event.

Remember, a plot consists of a series of events that are either **causes** or **effects.**

Plot
First event of the fairy tale:
Second event of the fairy tale:
Third event of the fairy tale:

Remember, when writing about events, use words such as **because, because of,** and **as a result of.**

Friendly Letter

Write a letter to a friend. First, **inform** him or her of the things you're doing. Then try to **persuade** him or her to join you to do something (perhaps to go on a trip or attend camp together). Use the words in the Word Boxes to strengthen your writing.

Words to Persuade	
please	again
to sum up	surely
definitely	why not?
try	only
the best	amazing
secondly	finally
even	

Words to Inform	
and then	such as
when	usually
so	here
for example	next
including	another

Writing

Writing to inform and persuade

Brain Box

Everything that is written has a purpose. The purpose could be to **inform, persuade,** or **entertain.** A written piece can have more than one purpose.

E-Mail

Write an e-mail to one of your favorite relatives. Entertain them by writing about something funny that happened to you or sharing a joke you heard.

Brain Box

You can add entertainment value to your writing by building suspense, saving the punch line for last, or using humorous language.

Japanese Poetry

Below is a **haiku** about autumn. Read it, then write a haiku about spring, summer, and winter below.

Leaves turning colors _____ 5 syllables

Dropping with each gust of wind _____ 7 syllables

Fall days come quickly _____ 5 syllables

_____ 5 syllables

_____ 7 syllables

_____ 5 syllables

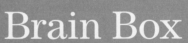

_____ 5 syllables

_____ 7 syllables

_____ 5 syllables

_____ 5 syllables

_____ 7 syllables

_____ 5 syllables

Writing

Writing a haiku

Brain Box

Haiku is a form of poetry from Japan. A haiku verse has a total of 17 syllables: 5 in the first line, 7 in the second and 5 in the third.

That's the Idea

Read about **idea webs**.

Tamara is using an **idea web** to help her write about her new closet. Each time she thinks of something to describe, she writes it in a small circle. She writes her **topic sentence** in the big circle.

shoe racks

pullout sweater shelf!

hooks for hats and bags

My new closet has special places for all my clothes.

two hanging rods, one above the other

My new closet has special places for all my clothes. All my sweaters go into a pullout shelf. My shoes go on a shoe rack, and my hats and bags go on special hooks. My new closet also has two hanging rods. One is above the other, so I can hang my pants on the bottom rod and my shirts on the top one. I love my new closet!

She uses her topic sentence as the first sentence of her paragraph. She uses each item in the smaller circles as supporting details.

Brain Box

An **idea web** can help you organize your thoughts before you start writing about a subject.

Pick a subject to write about. Make an **idea web** to help you brainstorm.

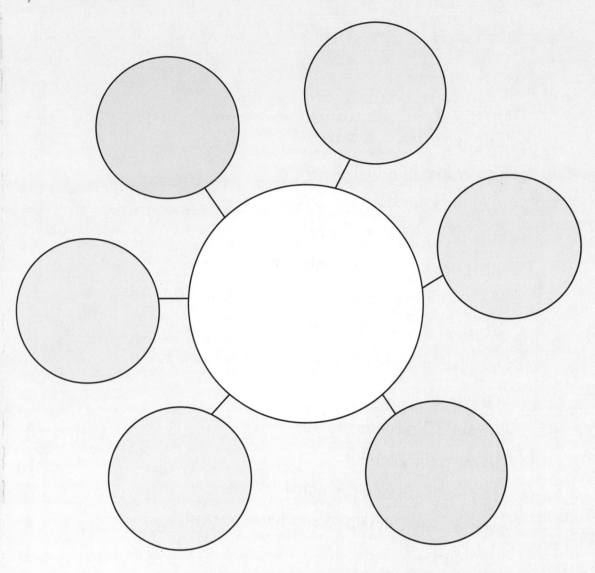

After you finish your idea web, write your paragraph below.

Taking Notes

Read the notes about the lynx, a type of wildcat.

– short tails

– long legs and big paws

– mostly live in forested areas

– very thick fur coat

– tufts of fur on tips of ears

– most are spotted for camouflage

– many live in North America, like Canada and Alaska

– mostly live in habitats that are cold and snow-covered

– about 30 pounds

– long, pointy teeth

– high-altitude environments

– some live in Russia, Scandinavia, parts of Europe

– most are light brown and gray

Writing

Idea web

Brain Box

Nonnarrative writing is writing that explains, reports, or informs. Examples of nonnarrative writing include journalism, research reports, recipes, and instruction manuals.

Nonnarrative writing usually requires taking **notes.** These are brief sentences written down to help you remember them later.

In the idea web below, give details telling what the lynx looks like and where the lynx lives. You can add as many circles as you want to the idea web. Write a topic sentence in the center circle.

Use your idea web to write a paragraph about the lynx. Begin your paragraph with the topic sentence in the center circle. Then use each smaller circle in your idea web as supporting details. Try to include as many supporting details as you can.

Badminton and Tennis

Read the notes in the **Venn diagram.**

This Venn diagram is about tennis and badminton, two sports that are alike but also have many differences.

BADMINTON
underhand serve
serve inside baseline
play with shuttlecock
shuttle must not bounce

BOTH
play with rackets
play on court
court has net
Olympic sports
2-person game or
4-person game

TENNIS
overhand serve
serve outside baseline
play with ball
ball may bounce

The blue circle lists all the things that are unique to badminton.

The pink circle lists all the things that are unique to tennis.

The part where the circle overlaps lists all the things the two have in common.

Brain Box

A **Venn diagram,** which is two circles that intersect, is a useful tool when comparing and contrasting subjects.

Use the notes in the Venn diagram to write two paragraphs comparing badminton and tennis. In the first paragraph, write about how the two sports are alike. In the second paragraph, write about how they differ from each other.

Writing

Comparing things

They're Connected

Read about what happened on December 16, 1773. Research the subject in an encyclopedia or on the Internet. List as many effects as you can on the page below.

Cause
On December 16, 1773, a group of American colonists dumped 342 tea chests from British ships into the waters of Boston Harbor.

Writing

Using cause and effect

Effects

Brain Box

Sometimes the things you write about are connected by **cause** and **effect**.

Be a Journalist

Write a **newspaper article** about Valdez the Vampire. Use the reporter's notes. Make sure you include the five W's.

Valdez the Vampire—Who

Called press conference—What

Going vegetarian, will drink only tomato juice, not blood—Why

Midnight, Friday, October 31—When

At Crumbling Castle, long believed to be haunted—Where

Brain Box

A newspaper article answers the five W's: **who, what, when, where,** and **why.**

Make Your Choice

Write a report.

Here are the first three steps to writing a good report:

1. **Choose a topic.** If you are given a topic, this step is already done. Otherwise, look for subject matter you are interested in.
2. **Do some quick research.** For quick research on a subject, a dictionary, encyclopedia, and the Internet are all excellent sources.
3. **Narrow your topic.** For example, if your topic was about dogs, you could narrow your topic to be just about a specific breed of dog.

Use this page to help you prepare to write your report. First choose a topic. Next do some quick research. Then narrow your topic to be about something specific. This is what your report will be about.

Writing

Narrowing a topic for a report

Topic
_____
_____
_____

Quick research
_____
_____
_____

Final topic of my report
_____
_____
_____

Now that you've chosen the final topic of your report, the next step is to do more research. In your research, keep two things in mind.

1. **Be sure to do enough research.** Use at least three different kinds of sources, such as an encyclopedia, a book specializing in the topic, a magazine article, or an interview with someone very knowledgeable on the subject.

   You can also research on the Internet. Just remember that Internet articles don't always give correct information, so you should try to verify the information by seeing if you can find similar information from a different source.

   Write a list of your research sources. Keep notes on who wrote the article and where the writers got their information.

   _____

   _____

   _____

   _____

How to research

2. **Take careful notes.** As you read through your research, write down important facts, quotations, or opinions on note cards or in a notebook.

   • Be sure to write the name of your source on each card or page.
   • Just write down the facts.
   • If you want to use an exact quotation, use quotation marks. Make sure to write down who the quotation is from.

Take Your Notes

Use these mini index cards to take notes as you research your report.

Writing

How to take
notes

Use as many cards as you need.
If you need more, use real
index cards.

Make Your Plan

Once you've finished your research, it's time to think about the best way to organize your report. Should it be in time order? Should it be comparison and contrast? Should it be cause and effect? Refer to your notes and choose a way to organize your report. Then fill in the idea webs below.

Remember to write each paragraph's main idea or topic sentence in the center circle, and the supporting details in the smaller circles.

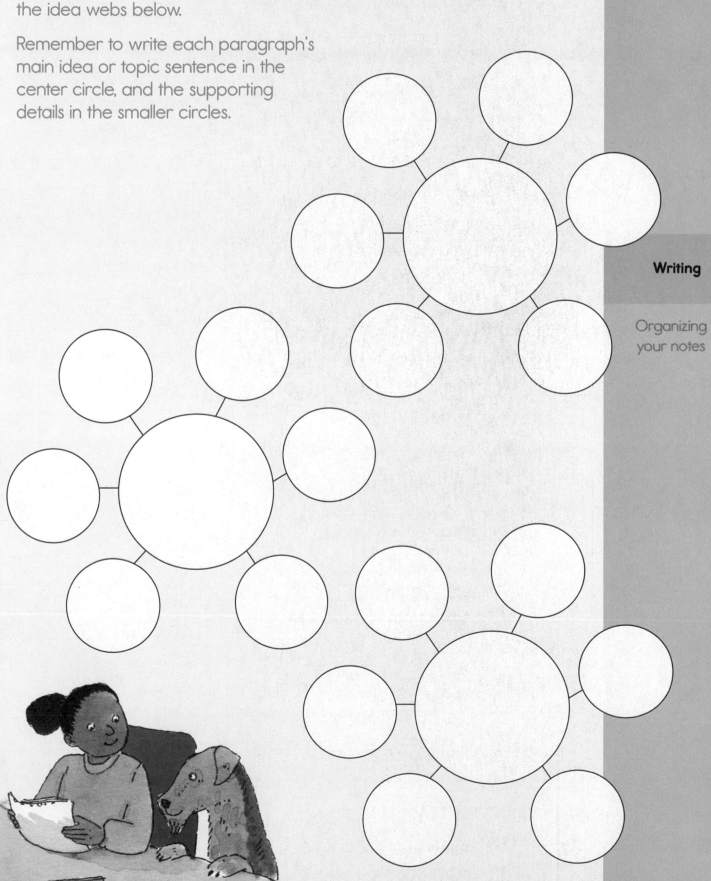

Prewrite Your Report

Once you've finished organizing your notes, it's time to **prewrite.**
Fill in the **outline** below using the information from your notes.

Topic:

1st Paragraph Topic Sentence:

1st Supporting Detail:

2nd Supporting Detail:

3rd Supporting Detail:

2nd Paragraph Topic Sentence:

1st Supporting Detail:

2nd Supporting Detail:

3rd Supporting Detail:

3rd Paragraph Topic Sentence:

1st Supporting Detail:

2nd Supporting Detail:

3rd Supporting Detail:

Writing

Prewriting

Brain Box

An **outline** is a way of organizing information by main idea and supporting details.

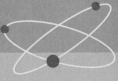

Your Final Report

Now write your final report. Remember to begin each paragraph with a topic sentence. Fill out your paragraphs with supporting details. Use interesting language and details in your writing.

To Be Exact

Write an **exact noun** for each general noun.

plant	_tulip_
dog	_____
celebrity	_____
vegetable	_____

Writing

Using exact nouns

Write six sentences, one for each **exact noun** in the Word Box. If you don't know what a word means, look it up in a dictionary.

surgeon	brook
gasoline	governor
telescope	lavender

Brain Box

An **exact noun** is a more precise form of a general noun.

Example:

A **doctor** is a **general noun**.

A **surgeon** is an **exact noun**.

In your writing, you can use exact nouns to make your sentences stronger.

Very Precise

Write a **vivid verb** for each general verb.

walk	_____
drive	_____
eat	_____
stir	_____

Write six sentences, one for each **vivid verb** in the Word Box. If you don't know what a word means, look it up in a dictionary.

| frowned | sniffed | yelped | signaled | fled | pondered |

Writing

Using vivid verbs

Brain Box

Use **vivid verbs** to make your writing come alive.
Example: He was **acting confused.**
He was **floundering.**

It's All in the Details

Make each sentence more interesting by rewriting it using your own **adjectives** and **adverbs**.

Luis painted a line on the sidewalk.

Luis quickly painted a blue line on the crooked sidewalk.

We took a walk.

My favorite shirt has a stripe.

Mom made an announcement.

Darla's dog looked at her.

The bike ride was bouncy.

I got drenched in the rain.

The weather is cold.

The spy studied the code.

Brain Box

Descriptive **words** such as **adjectives** and **adverbs** make your writing more interesting and more exact.

Put 'Em Together

Combine each set of sentences into one sentence. Use the words **because, but, and,** or **which;** use words in a series separated by **commas;** or change the order of the sentences if needed.

My dog is scratching himself. He has fleas.

My dog is scratching himself because he has fleas.

Kayla and Cyrah are friends. Kayla and Iniko are not friends.

I earn money by doing chores. My father pays me when I wash the car.

Many people live in China. This is why farming is so important in China.

My state has a state flower. It has a state bird and a state insect.

The name Mississippi means "great river." Native Americans named the Mississippi River. The Mississippi River is a powerful river.

Brain Quest Fourth Grade Workbook

Rewriting sentences

Writing

Brain Box

You can combine sentences to make your writing more interesting by:

- Joining two independent clauses with a conjunction such as **and, but,** or **because**

- Changing an independent clause into a dependent clause by adding the word **which**

- Writing words in a series separated by commas

U.S. Interstates

Rewrite this paragraph so it reads more smoothly. Combine the ten sentences into no more than five new sentences.

The directions of U.S. interstate highways are not hard to understand. They are easy to understand. All the even-numbered highways travel east. They also travel west. I-80 starts in New York City. I-80 ends up in San Francisco, California. All the odd-numbered highways run north. They run south as well. I-35 begins in Texas. It ends in Minnesota.

Writing

Combining sentences in paragraphs

On the Run

Correct each **run-on sentence** by rewriting it below.

The knight charged the castle, the drawbridge was going up.

The knight charged the castle because the drawbridge was going up.

Jeans are very popular, they are stylish and comfortable.

I don't like heights, we live on the 25th floor.

Gophers are cute, they are awesome diggers.

The planets travel around the sun, they travel in an ellipse, which is an oval shape.

Lance is a litterbug, he drops candy wrappers everywhere.

The remote control stopped working, its battery was dead.

Writing

Correcting run-on sentences

Brain Box

A **run-on sentence** can usually be corrected in two ways:

• Break the run-on sentences into two separate sentences

• Add a conjunction such as **and, but,** or **because**

Make It Smooth

Use the **transitional words** in the Word Box to rewrite this paragraph.

| first | next | then | another | second | third | finally |

To make a chocolate milk shake, you need milk, chocolate ice cream, and a blender. Put two scoops of ice cream in the blender. Add one-half cup of milk. Close the lid of the blender. (If you don't, you'll get milk everywhere!) Press the MIX button for six or seven seconds. Press the LIQUEFY button for another six or seven seconds. Take the lid off the blender. Pour the milk shake into a glass. Yum!

Writing

Using transitional words

Brain Box

Transitional words help make a smooth connection between one part of a sentence or paragraph to another.

Make the Mark

Here are some common **proofreading marks** you can learn and use.

Symbol	What it means	Example
a̲	capitalize	The pacific Ocean is the largest ocean in the world.
A̸	make lowercase	There are 25,000 Islands scattered throughout the ocean
∧/m	insert letter to spell correctly	The Pacific Ocean is so wide it touches the coasts of Indonesia and Colobia.
∧,	add a comma	It is home to incredible whales, sharks, and coral reefs.
⊙	add a period	The Pacific Ocean gets its name from the word for peaceful. It isn't always peaceful, though.
℘	delete or take out	The area the Pacific Ocean covers is bigger larger than the area covered by all the dry land on Earth.
¶	start a new paragraph	The Pacific Ocean has the deepest trenches in the world. ¶ The Indian Ocean is another beautiful Ocean.

Writing

Proofreading marks

Brain Box

Proofreading marks show what to correct when you edit.

Break It Up

Below is a single paragraph, but it contains three main ideas!
Underline the three topic sentences. Then write the correct
proofreading mark where each new **paragraph** should begin.

Digital photography is less expensive than film photography. With film photography, you must pay for the film, and then you pay to develop the film. Also, you must pay for each print that you want.  But with digital photography you don't buy film and you don't pay to develop the film. With digital photography it's easy to make changes in each photo. You can edit a photo to sharpen its focus. And you can add special effects to a photo. For example, you can tint it brown so that it looks old. Or you can crop it to get rid of unwanted things in the background. Digital photos can be used in many different ways. One way to use them is as screen savers. Another way is to make an electronic scrapbook of your digital photos. You can organize the photos in any order, as many times as you want. Best of all, you can e-mail digital photos to your friends!

Who Is Mark Twain?

Proofread the paragraph below using the correct **proofreading marks.** Then write the final draft on the lines below.

Samuel Langhorne Clemens grew up in Hannibal, missouri, in the 1840s and 1850s. when he was 12 years old, samuel became a printer's helper. he also rote newspaper stories

When he was 22 years old, Samuel clemens became a riverboat pilot on the mississippi river. It was important for pilots to know how deep the river was. When They shouted "mark twain," that meant the river was two fathoms deep

Later, Samuel Clemens became a writer. He took his name from the riverboat shout. that is how he became mark twain, author of *The adventures of Tom Sawyer*.

Writing

Using proofreading marks

Building Skills

Circle the **6** in each number and write its **place value.**

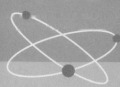

46 _____

614 _____

168 _____

4,602 _____

6,190 _____

6 _____

Math Skills

Place value

Circle the **1** in each number and write its place value.

1,542 _____

145 _____

4,321 _____

9,810 _____

Circle the **3** in each number and write its place value.

5,302 _____

9,143 _____

735 _____

3,447 _____

Brain Box

The **place value** of a digit in a number is determined by where it appears in the number.

Example: **2,547**

thousands	hundreds	tens	ones
2	5	4	7

Write It Out

Write out the **expanded notation** for each number.

	Thousands		Hundreds		Tens		Ones
5,147 =	5,000	+	100	+	40	+	7
7,975 =		+		+		+	
8,331 =		+		+		+	
2,784 =		+		+		+	
1,228 =		+		+		+	
6,977 =		+		+		+	
3,812 =		+		+		+	
8,429 =		+		+		+	
5,548 =		+		+		+	

Math Skills

Expanded and standard notation

Write the **standard notation** for each expanded notation below.

Ten Thousands		Thousands		Hundreds		Tens		Ones		
40,000	+	5,000	+	200	+	30	+	9	=	45,239
20,000	+	3,000	+	400	+	70	+	6	=	_____
50,000	+	7,000	+	500	+	50	+	7	=	_____
80,000	+	1,000	+	600	+	20	+	3	=	_____
40,000	+	6,000	+	900	+	50	+	8	=	_____
10,000	+	5,000	+	100	+	90	+	2	=	_____
30,000	+	2,000	+	800	+	30	+	9	=	_____
70,000	+	9,000	+	700	+	10	+	2	=	_____
90,000	+	4,000	+	300	+	40	+	4	=	_____
60,000	+	8,000	+	200	+	60	+	6	=	_____

Brain Box

The **standard notation** for a number is the way it is typically written.

Example: **2,736**

The **expanded notation** shows the place value of each digit in the number.

Example:
2,000 + 700 + 30 + 6

Rebel's Challenge

Rebel the computer has challenged Kyle to guess three different numbers. Read the clues and fill in the charts to find out Rebel's numbers.

> I'm thinking of a number that has 5 tens.
> It also has 9 thousands.
> And then, Kyle, it has 8 ten thousands!
> Also, it has 2 hundreds.
> Oh, yes—it has only 1 one.

Ten Thousands	Thousands	Hundreds	Tens	Ones	
					_____

Math Skills

Filling in place notation

> This is a new number, Kyle. It has 3 hundreds.
> It has 7 thousands.
> And it has 7 ones. I like 7s.
> The number I'm thinking of has 4 tens.
> It has as many ten thousands as it can, which is 9.

Ten Thousands	Thousands	Hundreds	Tens	Ones	
					_____

> Okay, here's your last number. It has 1 hundred.
> It has 2 ten thousands. It has 7 tens.
> I'm still thinking of my number.
> It has 6 ones.
> Only one place left, Kyle! It has 5 thousands.

Ten Thousands	Thousands	Hundreds	Tens	Ones	
					_____

Beach Ball Roundup

Round each number up or down. If you **round up** a number, write the answer in an inflated beach ball. If you **round down** a number, write the answer in a deflated beach ball.

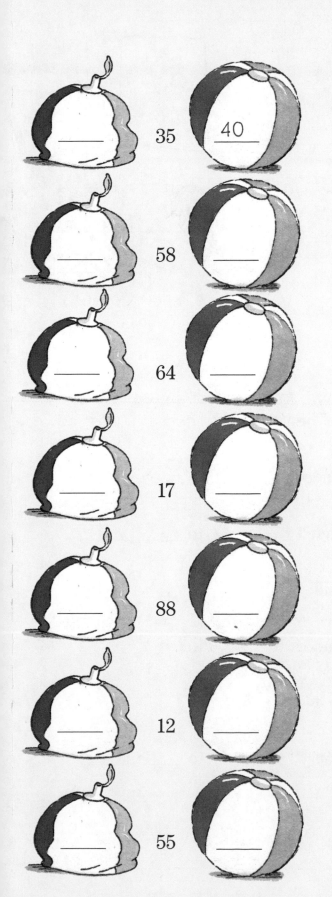

35 _____ 40

58 _____

64 _____

17 _____

88 _____

12 _____

55 _____

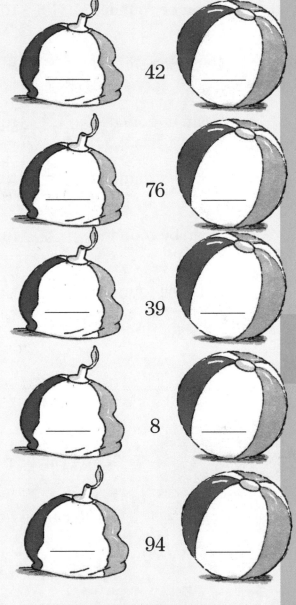

42 _____

76 _____

39 _____

8 _____

94 _____

Math Skills

Rounding tens

Brain Box

Numbers can be **rounded** to their next highest or next lowest place.

If the place you're rounding to is 5 or higher, you **round up**.

Example: **87** can be rounded up to become **90**

If the place you're rounding to is under 5, you **round down**.

Example: **82** can be **rounded down** to **80**

Up or Down

Round each number to its **nearest hundred**.
Write on the line whether you're rounding up or down.

689 can be rounded ___up___ to __700___ .

231 can be rounded _____ to _____ .

449 can be rounded _____ to _____ .

758 can be rounded _____ to _____ .

391 can be rounded _____ to _____ .

862 can be rounded _____ to _____ .

Rounding
hundreds and
thousands

Math Skills

Brain Box

When rounding to the **nearest hundred**, round up or down based on the number in the **tens place**. If the number is under 50, round down. If the number is 50 or higher, round up.

Example: **759** can be **rounded up** to **800**

When rounding to the **nearest thousand**, round up or down based on the number in the **hundreds place**. If the number is under 500, round down. If the number is 500 or higher, round up.

Example: **5,499** can be **rounded down** to **5,000**

Round each number to its **nearest thousand**.
Write on the line whether you're rounding up or down.

2,854 can be rounded _____ to _____ .

7,125 can be rounded _____ to _____ .

5,550 can be rounded _____ to _____ .

1,820 can be rounded _____ to _____ .

3,437 can be rounded _____ to _____ .

6,501 can be rounded _____ to _____ .

Round the Mountain

Round each number.

Round 784,392 to the nearest ten thousand: _____

Round 815,295 to the nearest thousand: _____

Round 98,670 to the nearest ten thousand: _____

Round 564,195 to the nearest hundred: _____

Round 1,643,253 to the nearest hundred thousand: _____

Round 3,845,211 to the nearest ten thousand: _____

Round 7,568,250 to the nearest hundred thousand: _____

Round 237,874 to the nearest thousand: _____

Round 598,587 to the nearest ten thousand: _____

Round 1,471,932 to the nearest hundred thousand: _____

Math Skills

Rounding

Brain Box

When rounding to the nearest **ten thousand,** round up or down based on the number in the **thousands place.** If the number is under 5,000, round down. If the number is 5,000 or higher, round up.

Example: **67,373** can be **rounded up** to **70,000**

When rounding to the nearest **hundred thousand,** round up or down based on the number in the **ten thousands place.** If the number is under 50,000, round down. If the number is 50,000 or higher, round up.

Example: **832,780** can be **rounded down** to **800,000**

Follow the Trail

Count by **tens.** Fill in the missing numbers.

5	15	25	35	45	55	65

Count by **fifteens.** Fill in the missing numbers.

20	___	___	___	___	95	___

Count by **twenties.** Fill in the missing numbers.

2	22	42	42	82	102	122	142

Count by **hundreds.** Fill in the missing numbers.

131	___	___	431	___
___	___	872	___	1,072
1,156	___	___	___	1,556
___	___	___	1,913	___

Math Skills

Skip counting

Count by **thousands.** Fill in the missing numbers.

7,742	___	___	10,742	___
___	41,891	42,891	___	___
33,220	___	___	___	37,220
___	___	___	99,633	___

Noted Numbers

Find the pattern. Fill in the missing numbers.

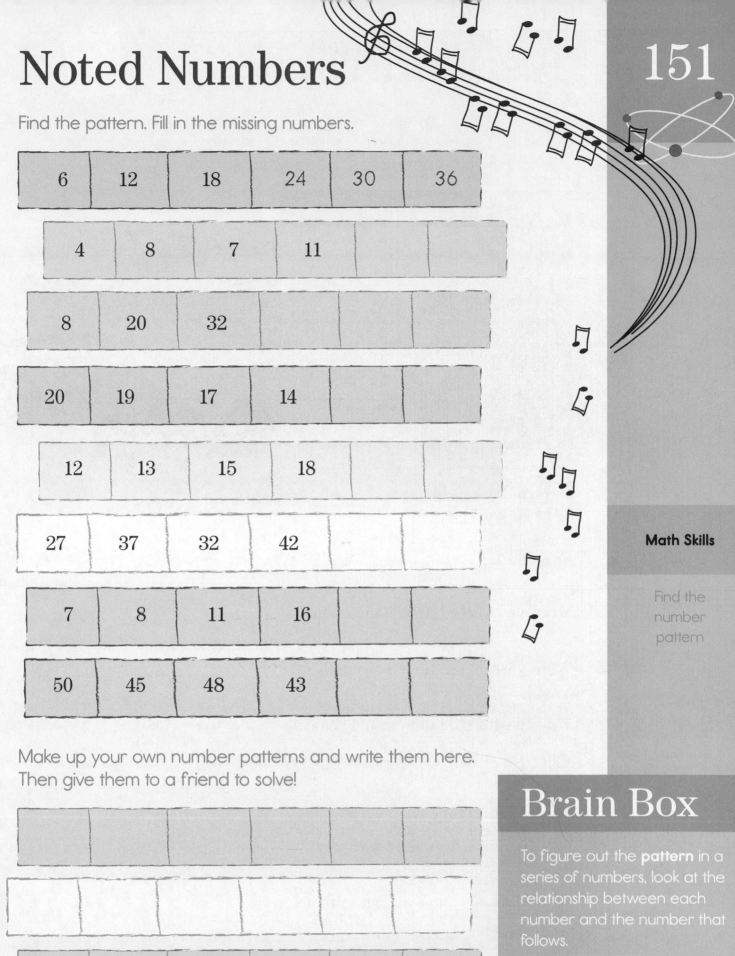

| 6 | 12 | 18 | 24 | 30 | 36 |

| 4 | 8 | 7 | 11 | | |

| 8 | 20 | 32 | | | |

| 20 | 19 | 17 | 14 | | |

| 12 | 13 | 15 | 18 | | |

| 27 | 37 | 32 | 42 | | |

| 7 | 8 | 11 | 16 | | |

| 50 | 45 | 48 | 43 | | |

Make up your own number patterns and write them here. Then give them to a friend to solve!

Math Skills

Find the number pattern

Brain Box

To figure out the **pattern** in a series of numbers, look at the relationship between each number and the number that follows.

Example: **8, 11, 9, 12, 10**

8	**11**	**9**	**12**	**10**
+3	−2	+3	−2	+3
11	9	12	10	13

The pattern for this number series is **+3, −2**. The next number would be 13.

Test-Run Time

Estimate how many minutes it will take each driver to finish the race based on the actual times of their test runs. Round up or down to the nearest ten. Then answer the questions that follow.

Name	Actual Time of Test Runs	Estimated Time
Helena	33	30
Graham	22	20
Victoria	27	30
Enzo	18	20
Kathleen	15	20
Pham	14	10
Morgan	36	40

Math Skills

Estimating numbers

Whose estimated time is the lowest? _pham_

Whose estimated time is the highest? _morgan_

Whose estimated time would change

if his test-run time had been one minute more? _pham_

Whose actual time was two minutes

less than his estimated time? _Enzo_

Whose actual time was four minutes

less than his estimated time? _morgan_

Brain Box

An **estimate** is an approximate number. One way to estimate a number is to round it up or down.

Just About Right

Estimate the sums by rounding each number to the nearest ten.

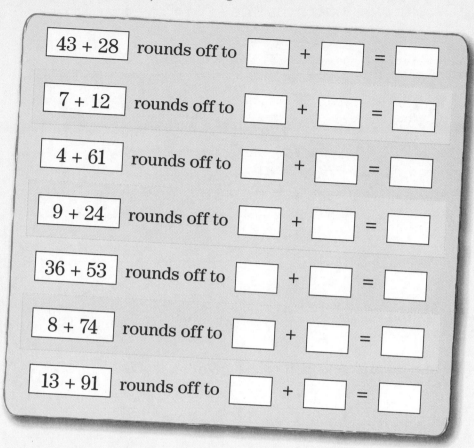

43 + 28   rounds off to ☐ + ☐ = ☐

7 + 12   rounds off to ☐ + ☐ = ☐

4 + 61   rounds off to ☐ + ☐ = ☐

9 + 24   rounds off to ☐ + ☐ = ☐

36 + 53   rounds off to ☐ + ☐ = ☐

8 + 74   rounds off to ☐ + ☐ = ☐

13 + 91   rounds off to ☐ + ☐ = ☐

Estimate the differences below by rounding each number to the nearest ten.

27 – 13   rounds off to ☐ – ☐ = ☐

51 – 33   rounds off to ☐ – ☐ = ☐

49 – 16   rounds off to ☐ – ☐ = ☐

34 – 19   rounds off to ☐ – ☐ = ☐

65 – 28   rounds off to ☐ – ☐ = ☐

91 – 39   rounds off to ☐ – ☐ = ☐

84 – 27   rounds off to ☐ – ☐ = ☐

Math Skills

Estimating
sums and
differences

In the Ballpark

Estimate the numbers in each problem to see if the answer is correct. Circle **Yes** if the answer looks right. Circle **No** if the answer looks wrong.

Math Skills

Using estimates to check answers

Michael adds 75 and 76 and gets 251. Yes No

Juan adds 89 and 34 and gets 123. Yes No

Ashley subtracts 42 from 85 and gets 43. Yes No

Nevaeh subtracts 17 from 99 and gets 52. Yes No

Caleb adds 53 to 51 and gets 144. Yes No

Jayla subtracts 24 from 71 and gets 47. Yes No

Christopher adds 62 to 44 and gets 106. Yes No

Megan subtracts 9 from 77 and gets 68. Yes No

Kioko adds 0 and 76 and gets 0. Yes No

John subtracts 53 from 84 and gets 31. Yes No

Brain Box

You can see if your answer looks correct by estimating before you solve a problem.

What's That Sign?

Write **<**, **>**, or **=** in each box to show the relationship between the sets of numbers.

10 + 11 ☐ 5 + 16   28 − 4 ☐ 18 + 10

4 − 1 ☐ 7 − 4   45 − 9 ☐ 6 × 6

7 + 8 ☐ 8 + 5   4 + 4 ☐ 4 × 4

2 + 13 ☐ 7 + 9

17 + 9 ☐ 28 − 5

10 + 2 ☐ 6 + 6

12 − 2 ☐ 9 + 9

Math Skills

Greater than, less than

Brain Box

In math:

• the symbol **<** means "less than."

• the symbol **>** means "greater than."

• the symbol **=** means "is the same as."

Roman Numerals

Look at the chart comparing **Arabic numbers** to **Roman numerals**.

1	2	3	4	5	6	7	8	9	10
I	II	III	IV	V	VI	VII	VIII	IX	X

20	50	100	500	1,000
XX	L	C	D	M

BRAIN FACT:
Mathematicians in India invented Arabic numerals 1,500 years ago!

Use the chart to write the Roman numeral equivalent to each number.

Math Skills

Roman numerals

3 = _____

53 = _____

5 = _____

24 = _____

10 = _____

157 = _____

8 = _____

521 = _____

20 = _____

1,555 = _____

Brain Box

The numerals we use to represent numbers are called **Arabic numbers.** **Roman numerals** use letters to represent numbers.

One and Itself

Follow the directions to learn the first four **prime numbers.**

1	2	3	4	5	6	7	8	9	10

Cross out the number 1. It is not a prime number.

Circle the number 2. It is the first prime number. It is also the only even prime number.

Look at the remaining numbers. Which of the remaining numbers have 2 as a factor? _____

Cross out these numbers. They are not prime numbers because they have other factors besides themselves and 1.
What numbers have not been crossed out? _____

One of these numbers has factors besides itself and 1.
What is that number? _____ Cross it out.

Circle the remaining numbers. They are prime numbers!

Math Skills

Prime
numbers

Now find the next group of prime numbers.

11	12	13	14	15	16	17	18	19	20

For the next 10 numbers, cross out every number that has 2 as a factor.

There are 5 numbers left. One of them has 3 and 5 as factors. Cross it out.

Circle the remaining numbers. They are prime numbers.

Write all the prime numbers from 2 to 20: _____

Brain Box

A **prime number** is a number greater than **1** whose factors can be divided evenly only by **1** and itself. For example, the number **3** is a prime number because its only factors are **3** and **1**. The number **4** is not a prime number, because it has four factors: **4** and **1**, and **2** and **2**.

Going Down

Write each amount as a **negative number.**

A diving chamber is two hundred feet below sea level. `-200`

The temperature is seventeen degrees below zero.

A submarine is three thousand,

one hundred and eighty-nine feet below the surface.

The scientists drilled one thousand

five hundred feet below sea level.

Math Skills

My brother isn't happy that

the temperature is twenty below.

Negative
numbers

Samantha owed her sister eighteen dollars and fifty cents

but didn't have any money in her piggy bank.

The nation's budget was in bad shape. The government

spent eight million dollars more than it had.

Brain Box

The numbers that we use most often are **positive numbers.** This means they are **greater than 0.**

Numbers **less than 0** are called **negative numbers.** A negative number always has a **minus sign** in front of it.

Example: **-20**

Left of Zero

Use the **number line** to answer the questions.

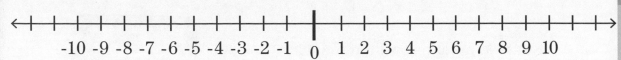

$$\begin{array}{ccccccccccccccccccccc} & -10 & -9 & -8 & -7 & -6 & -5 & -4 & -3 & -2 & -1 & 0 & 1 & 2 & 3 & 4 & 5 & 6 & 7 & 8 & 9 & 10 \end{array}$$

What number is four units to the right of 0? _____

What number is four units to the left of 0? _____

On the number line above, does every positive number have a matching negative number? _____

How many units from 0 is +5? _____

How many units from 0 is −5? _____

Math Skills

Negative numbers

If you stood on +3 and moved back 7 spaces to the left, where would you be? _____

If you stood on −5 and moved in a positive direction for 15 spaces, where would you be? _____

What is the opposite of +6? _____

How many units are there between +6 and its opposite? _____

On the number line above, write the numbers 11 and 12 and also −11 and −12.

Brain Box

A **number line** is a straight line that shows the relationship between numbers that are greater than and less than zero.

I Must Be Going

Write the correct time on each digital clock.

Seventeen minutes past ten o'clock

10 : 17

Fifteen minutes past twelve o'clock

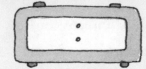

Half an hour past seven o'clock

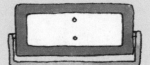

Twenty minutes before two o'clock

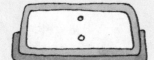

Math Skills

Nineteen minutes past eight o'clock

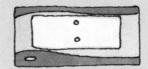

Time

Thirty-three minutes past ten o'clock

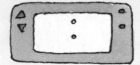

Ten minutes before six o'clock

Fifteen minutes before one o'clock

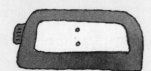

BRAIN FACT:
The first digital clock was invented in 1956!

Noon

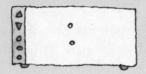

Half an hour before four o'clock

Addition and Subtraction

Heavy Lifting

Find the **sum.** Find the two heaviest weights and color them your favorite color.

Addition and Subtraction

Adding tens and hundreds

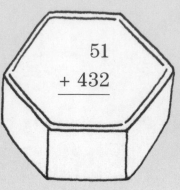

$$51 + 432$$

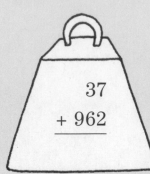

$$37 + 962$$

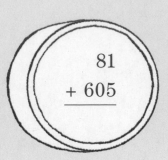

$$81 + 605$$

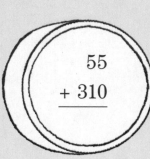

$$55 + 310$$

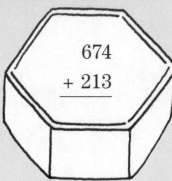

$$674 + 213$$

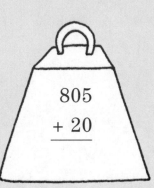

$$805 + 20$$

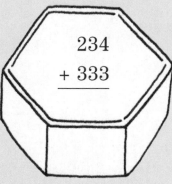

$$234 + 333$$

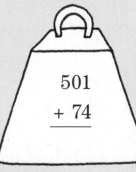

$$501 + 74$$

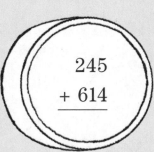

$$245 + 614$$

$$550 + 239$$

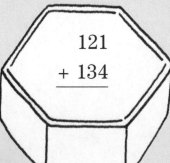

$$121 + 134$$

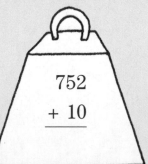

$$752 + 10$$

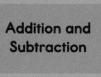

Favorite Number

Find the **sum.** Regroup if necessary. Now color all the tomato juice cans that add up to the same number red.

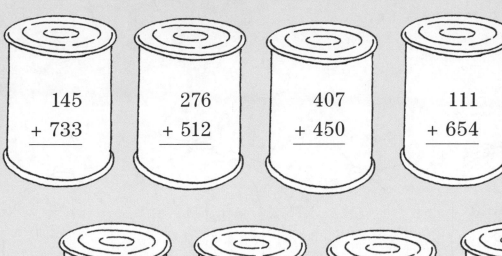

145
+ 733

276
+ 512

407
+ 450

111
+ 654

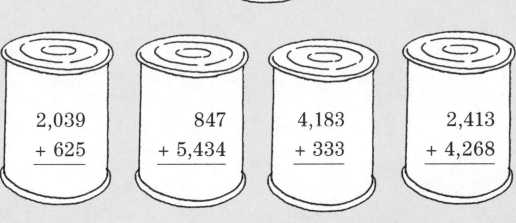

2,039
+ 625

847
+ 5,434

4,183
+ 333

2,413
+ 4,268

6,977
+ 2,045

1,287
+ 4,994

6,374
+ 1,998

5,172
+ 1,109

Addition and Subtraction

Adding hundreds and thousands

Sacks of Coins

Add the number of coins in each sack.
Color the sack that contains
the least amount of money red.
Color the sack that has the
most money green.

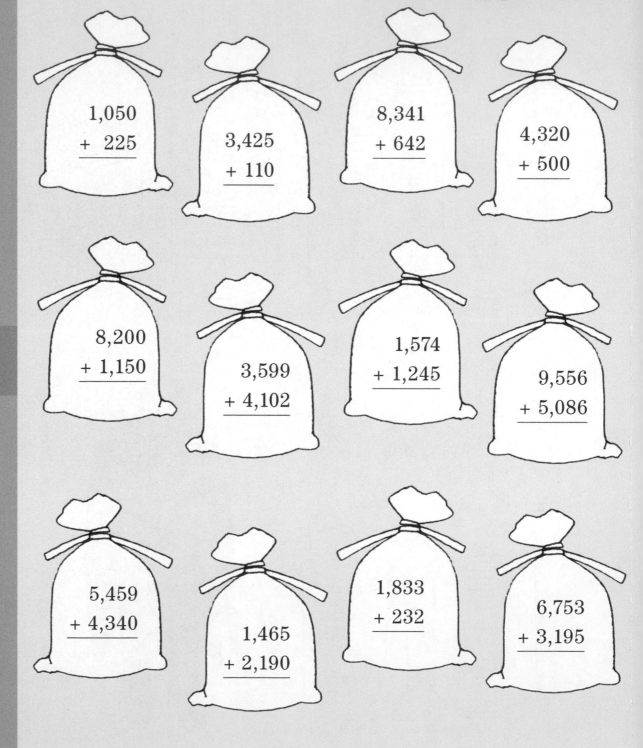

1,050
+ 225

3,425
+ 110

8,341
+ 642

4,320
+ 500

8,200
+ 1,150

3,599
+ 4,102

1,574
+ 1,245

9,556
+ 5,086

5,459
+ 4,340

1,465
+ 2,190

1,833
+ 232

6,753
+ 3,195

Heaviest Crate

Add the numbers to show how many pounds each crate weighs.
Circle the lightest crate. Draw an **X** through heaviest crate.

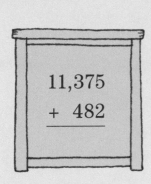

11,375
+   482
_____

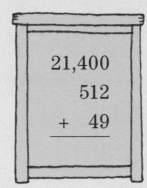

21,400
   512
+   49
_____

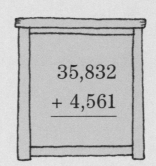

35,832
+ 4,561
_____

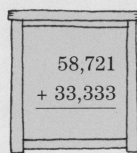

58,721
+ 33,333
_____

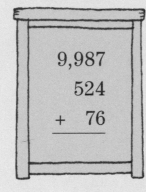

9,987
  524
+   76
_____

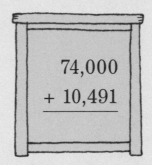

74,000
+ 10,491
_____

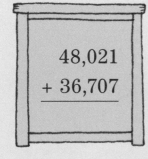

48,021
+ 36,707
_____

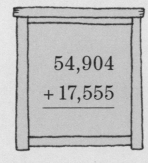

54,904
+ 17,555
_____

57,648
+ 5,976
_____

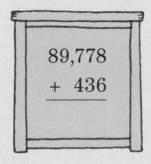

89,778
+   436
_____

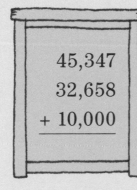

45,347
32,658
+ 10,000
_____

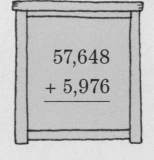

49,832
+ 22,301
_____

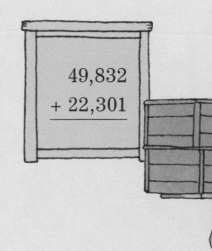

Hup, Two, Three!

Find the **difference.**

845
- 723

463
- 322

491
- 380

890
- 740

976
- 41

743
- 231

627
- 515

989
- 787

178
- 145

237
- 203

978
- 863

869
- 759

Write the highest number in the yellow box. _____

Write the lowest number in the pink box. _____

Subtract the lowest number from the highest
number. Write the number in the blue box. _____

Is this the quarterback's number? _____

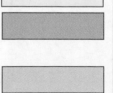

902

Mitten Mania

Find the **difference.** Regroup if necessary.

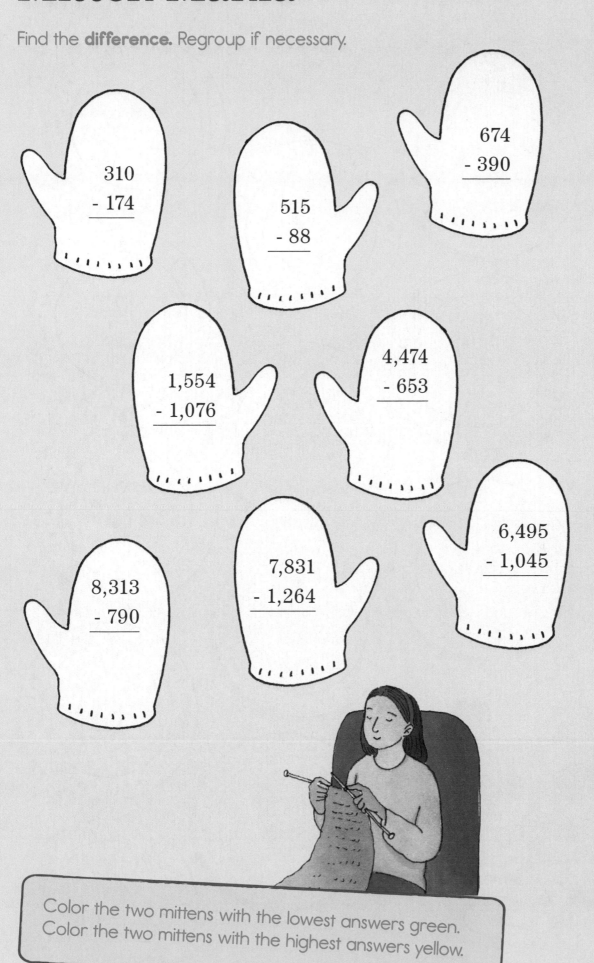

310
- 174
_____

515
- 88
_____

674
- 390
_____

1,554
- 1,076
_____

4,474
- 653
_____

8,313
- 790
_____

7,831
- 1,264
_____

6,495
- 1,045
_____

Color the two mittens with the lowest answers green.
Color the two mittens with the highest answers yellow.

Too Many Hot Dogs

Find the **difference**.

9,769
- 4,654

6,375
- 3,174

2,347
- 205

7,982
- 4,751

9,042
- 16

8,755
- 7,418

5,413
- 1,019

5,555
- 4,446

4,144
- 876

5,120
- 386

9,722
- 8,876

2,781
- 2,764

Too Much Hay

It's like looking for a needle in a haystack

Find the **difference.**

12,013
- 4,101

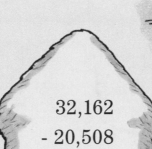
32,162
- 20,508

87,878
- 989

44,306
- 7,541

11,100
- 7,942

25,725
- 12,500

30,122
- 10,456

39,573
- 6,878

89,452
- 77,709

76,497
- 1,050

44,009
- 13,010

51,171
- 863

Plus or Minus

Find the **sum** or the **difference**.

10,500
+ 10,642

22,450
- 397

61,611
+ 5,720

9,873
+ 5,181

43,872
+ 33,422

55,982
+ 7,348

18,498
+ 2,450

99,999
- 68,789

24,600
- 4,654

52,000
- 45,370

10,500
- 3,075

48,756
+ 3,903

Multiplication and Division

Sets

Fill in the missing number to **multiply** each set.

2 × 2 = 4

4 × 2 = 6

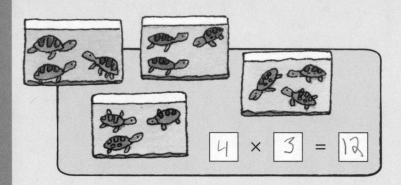

4 × 3 = 12

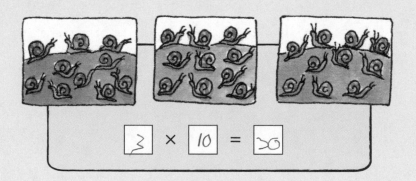

3 × 10 = 30

Multiplication and Division

Multiplying instead of adding

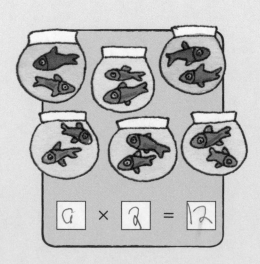

6 × 2 = 12

Brain Box

Multiplication is a quick way to find the sum of the same number added to itself.

Example:

3 + 3 + 3 + 3 = 12

3 × 4 = 12

Times Tables

Multiply.

$$\begin{array}{r} 2 \\ \times\ 2 \\ \hline 4 \end{array}$$
$$\begin{array}{r} 5 \\ \times\ 3 \\ \hline \end{array}$$
$$\begin{array}{r} 6 \\ \times\ 5 \\ \hline \end{array}$$
$$\begin{array}{r} 3 \\ \times\ 4 \\ \hline \end{array}$$
$$\begin{array}{r} 9 \\ \times\ 6 \\ \hline \end{array}$$

$$\begin{array}{r} 9 \\ \times\ 1 \\ \hline \end{array}$$
$$\begin{array}{r} 8 \\ \times\ 4 \\ \hline \end{array}$$
$$\begin{array}{r} 4 \\ \times\ 2 \\ \hline \end{array}$$
$$\begin{array}{r} 9 \\ \times\ 3 \\ \hline \end{array}$$
$$\begin{array}{r} 9 \\ \times\ 7 \\ \hline \end{array}$$

$$\begin{array}{r} 7 \\ \times\ 8 \\ \hline \end{array}$$
$$\begin{array}{r} 5 \\ \times\ 5 \\ \hline \end{array}$$
$$\begin{array}{r} 6 \\ \times\ 2 \\ \hline \end{array}$$
$$\begin{array}{r} 5 \\ \times\ 4 \\ \hline \end{array}$$
$$\begin{array}{r} 7 \\ \times\ 7 \\ \hline \end{array}$$

$$\begin{array}{r} 9 \\ \times\ 4 \\ \hline \end{array}$$
$$\begin{array}{r} 6 \\ \times\ 7 \\ \hline \end{array}$$
$$\begin{array}{r} 1 \\ \times\ 3 \\ \hline \end{array}$$
$$\begin{array}{r} 3 \\ \times\ 0 \\ \hline \end{array}$$

Multiplication and Division

Multiplying one-digit numbers

BRAIN FACT:
Any number multiplied by 0 is always 0!

BRAIN FACT:
Any number multiplied by 1 always stays the same!

The Facts About Factors

Fill in the missing **factors**.

$\underline{4} \times 8 = 32$ $6 \times \underline{} = 36$ $3 \times \underline{} = 15$

$\underline{} \times 7 = 49$ $4 \times \underline{} = 20$ $\underline{} \times \underline{} = 25$

Write all the possible factors for each number.

12

$1 \times 12 = 12$

$2 \times 6 = 12$

$3 \times 4 = 12$

$\underline{1} \quad \underline{12} \quad \underline{2}$

$\underline{6} \quad \underline{3} \quad \underline{4}$

9

_____

16

_____ _____

_____ _____ _____

15

_____ _____

_____ _____

18

_____ _____ _____

_____ _____ _____

8

_____ _____

_____ _____

Finish the math sentences.

The product of 5×8 is $\underline{40}$.

The product of 7×4 is _____.

The product of 9×2 is _____.

The product of 10×5 is _____.

The product of 2×11 is _____.

Brain Box

The two numbers in a multiplication problem
are called **factors**. The answer is the **product**.

Zeros

Multiply. Show your work.

20 × 3 —— 60	30 × 2	40 × 4	80 × 5	70 × 7
500 × 3	900 × 2	300 × 3	100 × 8	600 × 6
200 × 9	400 × 9	700 × 5	800 × 4	200 × 5
1,000 × 3	5,000 × 4	3,000 × 4	8,000 × 8	2,000 × 6
4,000 × 2	7,000 × 5	9,000 × 9	6,000 × 5	7,000 × 6

**Multiplication
and Division**

Multiplying by
zeros

Brain Box

When multiplying numbers ending in zero:

Multiply the ones, tens, and hundreds column in the usual order, from right to left.

Example: 400
         × 5
         ——
        2,000

or

Multiply the non-zero digits first.

Example: 400
         × 5
         ——
        2,000

Then count the numbers of zeros in the factors and add them to the end of the product.

Tens

Multiply. Regroup as needed. Show your work.

$$
\begin{array}{r}
\scriptstyle 3 \\
35 \\
\times\ 7 \\
\hline
245
\end{array}
$$

$$
\begin{array}{r}
72 \\
\times\ 2 \\
\hline
\end{array}
$$

$$
\begin{array}{r}
11 \\
\times\ 9 \\
\hline
\end{array}
$$

$$
\begin{array}{r}
48 \\
\times\ 6 \\
\hline
\end{array}
$$

$$
\begin{array}{r}
93 \\
\times\ 4 \\
\hline
\end{array}
$$

$$
\begin{array}{r}
19 \\
\times\ 7 \\
\hline
\end{array}
$$

$$
\begin{array}{r}
37 \\
\times\ 6 \\
\hline
\end{array}
$$

$$
\begin{array}{r}
90 \\
\times\ 8 \\
\hline
\end{array}
$$

$$
\begin{array}{r}
53 \\
\times\ 7 \\
\hline
\end{array}
$$

$$
\begin{array}{r}
22 \\
\times\ 5 \\
\hline
\end{array}
$$

$$
\begin{array}{r}
84 \\
\times\ 3 \\
\hline
\end{array}
$$

$$
\begin{array}{r}
89 \\
\times\ 4 \\
\hline
\end{array}
$$

$$
\begin{array}{r}
58 \\
\times\ 8 \\
\hline
\end{array}
$$

$$
\begin{array}{r}
34 \\
\times\ 6 \\
\hline
\end{array}
$$

$$
\begin{array}{r}
71 \\
\times\ 9 \\
\hline
\end{array}
$$

$$
\begin{array}{r}
33 \\
\times\ 4 \\
\hline
\end{array}
$$

$$
\begin{array}{r}
77 \\
\times\ 4 \\
\hline
\end{array}
$$

$$
\begin{array}{r}
25 \\
\times\ 1 \\
\hline
\end{array}
$$

$$
\begin{array}{r}
12 \\
\times\ 9 \\
\hline
\end{array}
$$

$$
\begin{array}{r}
67 \\
\times\ 3 \\
\hline
\end{array}
$$

Multiplication and Division

Multiplying two digits by one digit

Brain Box

When you multiply, you might need to **regroup.** Here's how to regroup **tens.**

Step 1: Multiply the number in the ones place and regroup.

Example:

$$
\begin{array}{r}
\scriptstyle 2 \\
2\,3 \\
\times\ 8 \\
\hline
4
\end{array}
$$

$3 \times 8 = 24$

3 times 8 is 24, so you write the 4 in the ones column, and carry the 2 into the 10s column.

Step 2: Multiply the number in the tens column. Add the number carried over.

Example:

$$
\begin{array}{r}
\scriptstyle 2 \\
2\,3 \\
\times\ 8 \\
\hline
184
\end{array}
$$

$2 \times 8 + 2 = 18$

2 times 8 is 16. 16 plus 2 is 18.

Hundreds

Multiply. **Regroup** as needed. Show your work.

$$
\begin{array}{r}
\scriptstyle 1\ 1 \\
233 \\
\times\ 6 \\
\hline
1{,}398
\end{array}
\qquad
\begin{array}{r}
190 \\
\times\ 4 \\
\hline
\end{array}
\qquad
\begin{array}{r}
312 \\
\times\ 9 \\
\hline
\end{array}
\qquad
\begin{array}{r}
253 \\
\times\ 7 \\
\hline
\end{array}
\qquad
\begin{array}{r}
384 \\
\times\ 3 \\
\hline
\end{array}
$$

$$
\begin{array}{r}
343 \\
\times\ 6 \\
\hline
\end{array}
\qquad
\begin{array}{r}
190 \\
\times\ 8 \\
\hline
\end{array}
\qquad
\begin{array}{r}
512 \\
\times\ 9 \\
\hline
\end{array}
\qquad
\begin{array}{r}
653 \\
\times\ 5 \\
\hline
\end{array}
\qquad
\begin{array}{r}
433 \\
\times\ 8 \\
\hline
\end{array}
$$

$$
\begin{array}{r}
946 \\
\times\ 8 \\
\hline
\end{array}
\qquad
\begin{array}{r}
264 \\
\times\ 7 \\
\hline
\end{array}
\qquad
\begin{array}{r}
326 \\
\times\ 7 \\
\hline
\end{array}
\qquad
\begin{array}{r}
342 \\
\times\ 9 \\
\hline
\end{array}
\qquad
\begin{array}{r}
584 \\
\times\ 8 \\
\hline
\end{array}
$$

Multiplication and Division

Multiplying three digits by one digit

Brain Box

Here's how to regroup **hundreds**.

Example:	Step 1:	Step 2:	Step 3:
$\begin{array}{r}\scriptstyle 4\ 5\\ \mathbf{268}\\ \times\ \mathbf{7}\\ \hline 1{,}876\end{array}$	Multiply ones and regroup.	Multiply tens, add, and regroup.	Multiply hundreds and add.
	$8 \times 7 = 56$	$6 \times 7 + 5 = 47$	$2 \times 7 + 4 = 18$

Two's Company

Multiply. **Regroup** as needed. Show your work.

22 × 33 ¹66 660 726	15 × 11	61 × 37	40 × 10	41 × 12
23 × 32	14 × 21	58 × 10	11 × 13	91 × 15

The aquarium has 27 tanks of tropical fish. Each tank contains 17 fish. How many tropical fish does the aquarium have in all?

Brain Box

Here's how you multiply two-digit numbers:

Example:
46
×12

Step 1:
Multiply the ones. Regroup.

¹
46
×12
92

Step 2: Put a 0 in the ones column.

46
×12
92
0

Step 3:
Multiply the tens column.

46
×12
92
460

Step 4:
Add the two products.

46
×12
¹92
+ 460
552

Cheering Section

Multiply. **Regroup** as needed. Show your work.

```
  1
 13
 56
× 35
 1
 280
1,680
1,960
```

```
  84
× 30
```

```
  39
× 91
```

```
  36
× 15
```

```
  58
× 67
```

```
  45
× 26
```

```
  72
× 34
```

```
  37
× 59
```

```
  63
× 42
```

```
  44
× 53
```

```
  75
× 68
```

```
  69
× 59
```

Mia collects pom-poms. She just bought 19 boxes of pom-poms. Each box contains 12 pom-poms. How many pom-poms has she added to her collection?

_____

Three Levels

Multiply. **Regroup** as needed. Show your work.

$$
\begin{array}{r}
234 \\
\times\ 21 \\
\hline
{}^{1}234 \\
4{,}680 \\
\hline
4{,}914 \\
\end{array}
$$

$$
\begin{array}{r}
158 \\
\times\ 72 \\
\hline
\end{array}
$$

$$
\begin{array}{r}
541 \\
\times\ 77 \\
\hline
\end{array}
$$

$$
\begin{array}{r}
639 \\
\times\ 35 \\
\hline
\end{array}
$$

$$
\begin{array}{r}
310 \\
\times\ 44 \\
\hline
\end{array}
$$

$$
\begin{array}{r}
605 \\
\times\ 47 \\
\hline
\end{array}
$$

$$
\begin{array}{r}
578 \\
\times\ 19 \\
\hline
\end{array}
$$

$$
\begin{array}{r}
753 \\
\times\ 58 \\
\hline
\end{array}
$$

Chef Chanticleer has 103 very hungry people to cook for. He cooks a dozen eggs for each person. How many eggs does the chef cook in all?

_____

Multiplication and Division

Multiplying three-digit numbers with regrouping

Brain Box

Here's how to multiply a three-digit number by a two-digit number:

Example:

$$
\begin{array}{r}
{}^{32} \\
{}^{11} \\
454 \\
\times\ 63 \\
\hline
{}^{1}\ \ \ \\
1{,}362 \\
+\ 27{,}240 \\
\hline
28{,}602 \\
\end{array}
$$

Step 1: Multiply the three-digit number by the number in the ones column. Regroup as needed.

Step 2: Add a zero to the bottom of the ones column. Then multiply the three-digit number by the number in the tens column.

Step 3: Add.

First Division

Fill in the boxes to write the **division** problems both ways.
Write the answer, too.

$12 \div 4 = 3$

$4 \overline{)12}$ with 3 on top

$9 \div 3 = \square$

$3 \overline{)9}$

$21 \div 3 = \square$

$\square \overline{)\square}$

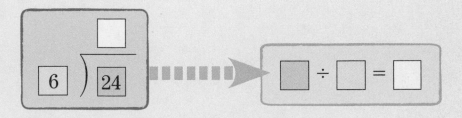

$6 \overline{)24}$

$\square \div \square = \square$

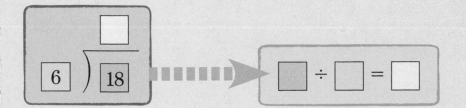

$6 \overline{)18}$

$\square \div \square = \square$

Multiplication and Division

Division

Brain Box

Division is the opposite of multiplication. It's the process of finding out how many times one number will fit into another number.

A division problem can be written two ways:

$15 \div 3 = 5$ $3 \overline{)15}$ with 5 on top

Cricket Division

Divide to find the **quotient**.

```
  11
5)55
  5↓
  05
   5
   0
```

```
    6
3)18
```

```
   10
6)60
```

```
    5
4)20
```

```
    1
8)88
```

```
2)46
```

```
7)70
```

```
7)56
```

```
2)68
```

```
3)21
```

Divide to find the quotient.

$49 \div 7 =$ _____ $25 \div 5 =$ _____

$63 \div 9 =$ _____ $36 \div 4 =$ _____

$56 \div 8 =$ _____ $27 \div 3 =$ _____

Dividing one-digit numbers into two-digit numbers

Multiplication and Division

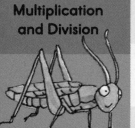

Brain Box

The number being divided is called the **dividend.** The number being divided into it is called the **divisor.** The answer to a division problem is called the **quotient.**

```
         13 ←——— quotient
divisor →4)52 ←dividend
```

```
dividend→ 52 ÷ 4 = 13←quotient
                      ↖divisor
```

To find the quotient in a division problem: | Example: 4)52

Step 1: Divide into the tens.

```
   1
4)52
  1
4)52
```

Step 2: Subtract.

```
   1
4)52
  -4
   1
```

Step 3: Bring down the ones.

```
   1
4)52
  -4↓
   12
```

Step 4: Divide into the new number.

```
  13
4)52
 -4
  12
```

If the divisor is larger than the first digit of the dividend, divide it into two digits, not one. For example:

```
   8
4)32
```

What Remains

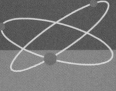

Divide. Show your work. Write the **remainder** next to the **r.**

$$\begin{array}{r} 12\text{ r }1 \\ 4\overline{)49} \\ -4\downarrow \\ \hline 09 \\ -8 \\ \hline \textcircled{1} \end{array}$$

$2\overline{)13}\ {}^{\text{r}}$ $7\overline{)60}\ {}^{\text{r}}$ $5\overline{)11}\ {}^{\text{r}}$ $8\overline{)21}\ {}^{\text{r}}$

$3\overline{)74}\ {}^{\text{r}}$ $4\overline{)55}\ {}^{\text{r}}$ $8\overline{)75}\ {}^{\text{r}}$ $6\overline{)34}\ {}^{\text{r}}$ $7\overline{)41}\ {}^{\text{r}}$

$6\overline{)64}\ {}^{\text{r}}$ $8\overline{)99}\ {}^{\text{r}}$ $9\overline{)33}\ {}^{\text{r}}$ $4\overline{)75}\ {}^{\text{r}}$ $7\overline{)79}\ {}^{\text{r}}$

Dividing one-digit numbers into two-digit numbers with remainders

Multiplication and Division

Brain Box

Sometimes the divisor doesn't go into the dividend evenly. Then you have a number left over. This number is called the **remainder.**

Example:

The answer is 13 r 3 (**r** for **remainder**).

$$\begin{array}{r} 13\ \textcircled{r 3} \\ 6\overline{)81} \\ -6 \\ \hline 21 \\ -18 \\ \hline 3 \end{array}$$

Check It Out!

```
      18r1        2
   3)55         18
    - 3↓        × 3
      25         54
    - 24        + 1
       1         55
```

$2)\overline{71}$

$5)\overline{79}$

$8)\overline{63}$

$6)\overline{51}$

$9)\overline{95}$

Multiplication and Division

Checking your answer

$8)\overline{76}$

$4)\overline{49}$

$7)\overline{87}$

Brain Box

You can check the answer to a division problem by multiplying. First, **multiply** the **quotient** by the divisor. Then, **add** any remainder. The number you get should be the same as the dividend.

Sock Drawer

Divide. Show your work.

```
   166
2)332
 - 2↓
   13
 -  12
    12
```

```
5)840
```

```
7)432
```

```
6)111
```

```
4)272
```

```
3)515
```

```
8)195
```

```
9)476
```

```
5)183
```

Glow-Glow has 789 T-shirts to put on sale in three different stores. How many shirts will it give to each store?

Dividing one-digit numbers into three-digit numbers

Multiplication and Division

Brain Box

When dividing a three-digit number by a one-digit number:

Step 1: Divide into the hundreds.

Step 2: Subtract.

Step 3: Bring down the tens and then divide into the tens.

Step 4: Subtract again.

Step 5: Bring down the ones and divide into the ones.

Step 6: If there is a remainder, write it next to the answer.

Example:
```
    172 r1
3)517
 -3↓
   21
 - 21↓
    07
   - 6
     1
```

Missing Signs

Look at each problem and fill in the missing **+**, **−**, **×**, or **÷** sign.

264 $\boxed{\div}$ 3 = 88

20 $\boxed{\times}$ 6 = 120

549 $\boxed{-}$ 510 = 39

28 $\boxed{\times}$ 12 = 336

18 $\boxed{+}$ 45 = 63

645 $\boxed{+}$ 130 = 775

99 $\boxed{-}$ 55 = 44

89 $\boxed{+}$ 21 = 110

123 $\boxed{-}$ 5 = 118

Multiplication and Division

Add, subtract, multiply, or divide

567 $\boxed{\div}$ 7 = 81

167 $\boxed{-}$ 92 = 75

375 $\boxed{\div}$ 5 = 75

My Dear Aunt Sally

Solve the following problems by using the correct **order of operations**.

$4 + 4 \times 5 = \quad 4 + 20 = 24$

20

$8 + 7 \times 2 =$

$12 + 18 \div 3 =$

$5 \times 3 - 11 =$

Dividing two-digit numbers into three-digit numbers

Multiplication and Division

$24 \div 8 + 4 - 7 =$

$47 - 9 \times 4 =$

Brain Box

Order of operations tells you the order in which you should solve a math problem with multiple steps: **M**ultiply, **D**ivide, **A**dd, and **S**ubtract. Use the phrase: "**M**y **D**ear **A**unt **S**ally" to help remember the correct order.

In the Middle

Find the **average** of each group of numbers.

	Sum	Average	Work Space
11 + 7 + 18 =	<u>36</u>	<u>12</u>	36 ÷ 3 = 12
37 + 55 =	___	___	
8 + 15 + 9 + 12 =	___	___	
374 + 156 =	___	___	
20 + 60 + 80 + 120 =	___	___	
19 + 27 + 32 =	___	___	
114 + 264 =	___	___	
32 + 56 + 87 + 97 =	___	___	
99 + 77 + 154 =	___	___	
6 + 10 + 18 + 18 =	___	___	

Multiplication and Division

Averaging

Brain Box

You can find an **average** by adding the group of numbers and then dividing the sum by the number of numbers in the group.

Example: **7, 12, 5, 12**

Step 1: **7 + 12 + 5 + 12 = 36**

Step 2: **36 ÷ 4 = 9**

9 is the **average**

I have a good average.

Fractions and Decimals

Parts of a Whole

Write a **fraction** to show which part of each whole is shaded.

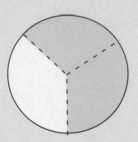

$$\frac{2}{3}$$

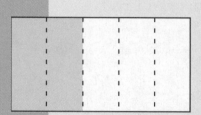

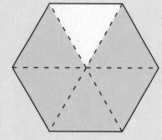

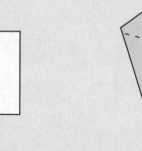

Fractions and Decimals

Identifying numerators and denominators

Brain Box

A **fraction** shows parts of a whole. Fractions are written as one number on top of another, with a line between them.

Example:

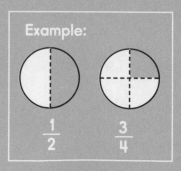

$$\frac{1}{2} \qquad \frac{3}{4}$$

The bottom number of a fraction is called the **denominator.** It tells the total number of pieces in the whole. The top number is the **numerator.** It tells how many pieces of the whole you are talking about.

Name the Part

Fill in the missing **numerator** or **denominator** for each fraction.

$\dfrac{4}{\boxed{7}}$

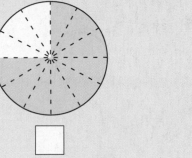

$\dfrac{\boxed{}}{12}$

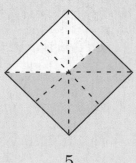

$\dfrac{5}{\boxed{}}$

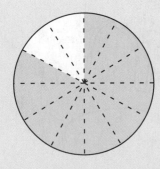

$\dfrac{7}{\boxed{}}$

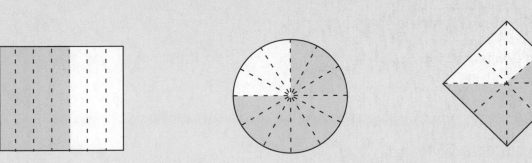

$\dfrac{4}{\boxed{}}$

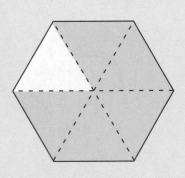

$\dfrac{\boxed{}}{6}$

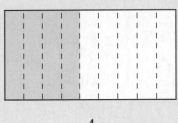

$\dfrac{10}{\boxed{}}$

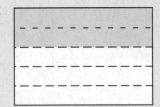

$\dfrac{\boxed{}}{5}$

Fractions and Decimals

Identifying numerators and denominators

Thomas cut a round birthday cake into eight pieces. He ate three of the pieces. Write a fraction to show what part of the cake Thomas ate.

$\dfrac{\boxed{}}{\boxed{}}$

Up the Ladder

Add the fractions.

HINT: Sometimes it helps to draw your own shaded diagrams to help you add fractions.

10/10
9/10
8/10
7/10
6/10
5/10
4/10
3/10
2/10
1/10

Adding
fractions

**Fractions and
Decimals**

$$\frac{1}{3} + \frac{1}{3} = \frac{2}{3}$$

$$\frac{1}{4} + \frac{2}{4} = \frac{\square}{\square}$$

$$\frac{1}{5} + \frac{1}{5} = \frac{\square}{\square}$$

$$\frac{1}{6} + \frac{2}{6} = \frac{\square}{\square}$$

$$\frac{1}{7} + \frac{5}{7} = \frac{\square}{\square}$$

$$\frac{1}{8} + \frac{6}{8} = \frac{\square}{\square}$$

$$\frac{1}{10} + \frac{6}{10} = \frac{\square}{\square}$$

$$\frac{1}{12} + \frac{8}{12} = \frac{\square}{\square}$$

Fill in the missing **numerator** or **denominator** for each problem.

$$\frac{\square}{10} + \frac{6}{10} = \frac{7}{10}$$

$$\frac{3}{8} + \frac{\square}{\square} = \frac{5}{8}$$

$$\frac{1}{\square} + \frac{1}{\square} = \frac{2}{4}$$

$$\frac{\square}{\square} + \frac{1}{3} = \frac{2}{3}$$

$$\frac{3}{7} + \frac{1}{\square} = \frac{4}{7}$$

$$\frac{1}{6} + \frac{\square}{\square} = \frac{3}{\square}$$

$$\frac{2}{5} + \frac{\square}{5} = \frac{3}{\square}$$

$$\frac{1}{\square} + \frac{6}{12} = \frac{7}{\square}$$

Brain Box

You can add fractions with the same **denominators** by adding the **numerators.** Their sum becomes the new numerator. The denominator remains the same.

Example:

$$\frac{1}{6} + \frac{4}{6} = \frac{5}{6}$$

Fraction Frenzy

Subtract the fractions.

$$\frac{2}{3} - \frac{1}{3} = \frac{\boxed{}}{\boxed{}}$$

$$\frac{4}{5} - \frac{2}{5} = \frac{\boxed{}}{\boxed{}}$$

$$\frac{5}{7} - \frac{1}{7} = \frac{\boxed{}}{\boxed{}}$$

$$\frac{9}{12} - \frac{7}{12} = \frac{\boxed{}}{\boxed{}}$$

$$\frac{7}{8} - \frac{5}{8} = \frac{\boxed{}}{\boxed{}}$$

$$\frac{4}{6} - \frac{3}{6} = \frac{\boxed{}}{\boxed{}}$$

$$\frac{13}{15} - \frac{7}{15} = \frac{\boxed{}}{\boxed{}}$$

$$\frac{8}{9} - \frac{5}{9} = \frac{\boxed{}}{\boxed{}}$$

$$\frac{3}{4} - \frac{2}{4} = \frac{\boxed{}}{\boxed{}}$$

$$\frac{7}{10} - \frac{1}{10} = \frac{\boxed{}}{\boxed{}}$$

Candice cut a rectangular birthday cake into 16 pieces. Her brother and sister ate a total of 5 pieces. Write a fraction to show what part of Candice's cake was left.

Fractions and Decimals

Subtracting fractions

Brain Box

You can **subtract** fractions with the same denominator by subtracting the numerators. The denominator will remain the same.

Example: $\frac{5}{7} - \frac{2}{7} = \frac{3}{7}$

In the Shade

Look at the shape and fraction on each card. Circle the shape that shows an **equivalent fraction.** Write that equivalent in the box.

 $\dfrac{1}{3}$ = $\dfrac{2}{6}$

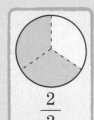 $\dfrac{2}{3}$ = $\dfrac{}{}$

 $\dfrac{1}{2}$ =  $\dfrac{}{}$

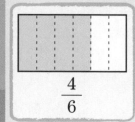 $\dfrac{4}{6}$ = 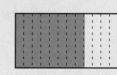  $\dfrac{}{}$

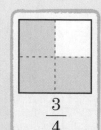 $\dfrac{3}{4}$ = $\dfrac{}{}$

Fractions and Decimals

Identifying equivalent fractions

Brain Box

Fractions that stand for the same amount are called **equivalent fractions.** Look at the shaded parts.

Example: $\dfrac{1}{2}$ is equivalent to $\dfrac{2}{4}$

Whole Parts

Write the **number 1 as a fraction** using each figure.

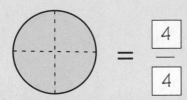 = $\dfrac{4}{4}$ 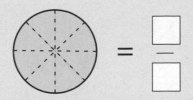 = $\dfrac{\square}{\square}$

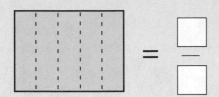 = $\dfrac{\square}{\square}$ 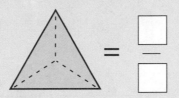 = $\dfrac{\square}{\square}$

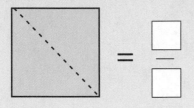 = $\dfrac{\square}{\square}$ 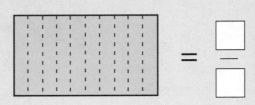 = $\dfrac{\square}{\square}$

195

Brain Box

When 1 is written as a fraction, the numerator and denominator are equal.

Example: $\dfrac{2}{2}$ and $\dfrac{3}{3}$

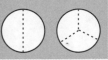

Equivalent fractions are two different fractions that show the same number.

Example: $\dfrac{4}{8}$

and

$\dfrac{1}{2}$

You can find an equivalent fraction by multiplying the numerator and the denominator by the same number.

Fractions and Decimals

Equivalent fractions

Fill in the missing parts.

$\dfrac{2}{5} \times \dfrac{\boxed{2}}{\boxed{2}} = \dfrac{4}{10}$ $\dfrac{1}{7} \times \dfrac{2}{2} = \dfrac{\square}{\square}$

$\dfrac{1}{2} \times \dfrac{4}{4} = \dfrac{\square}{\square}$ $\dfrac{4}{5} \times \dfrac{3}{3} = \dfrac{\square}{\square}$

$\dfrac{3}{6} \times \dfrac{\square}{\square} = \dfrac{6}{12}$ $\dfrac{3}{8} \times \dfrac{\square}{\square} = \dfrac{6}{16}$

$\dfrac{1}{3} \times \dfrac{\square}{\square} = \dfrac{3}{9}$ $\dfrac{2}{4} \times \dfrac{2}{2} = \dfrac{\square}{\square}$

HINT:
Remember that any number multiplied by one always stays the same. 1 written as a fraction can be $\dfrac{1}{1}$ or $\dfrac{2}{2}$ or $\dfrac{3}{3}$, etc.

Up, Up, Up!

Fill in the boxes to find an **equivalent fraction** with the denominator of **12**.

$$\frac{2}{3} \times \frac{4}{4} = \frac{8}{12}$$

$$\frac{2}{4} \times \frac{3}{3} = \frac{6}{12} = \frac{2}{4}$$

$$\frac{4}{4} \times \frac{3}{3} = \frac{12}{12}$$

$$\frac{5}{6} \times \frac{2}{2} = \frac{10}{12}$$

Fractions and Decimals

Putting fractions in ascending order

$$\frac{1}{6} \times \frac{2}{2} = \frac{2}{12} = \frac{2}{6}$$

$$\frac{1}{3} \times \frac{4}{4} = \frac{4}{12} \quad \frac{3}{6}$$

First write equivalent fractions in order from smallest to largest.
Then write the original fractions in order from smallest to largest.

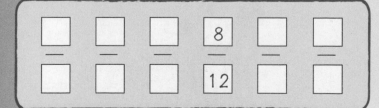

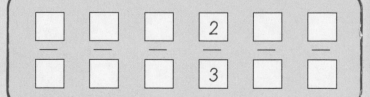

Musical Numbers

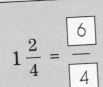

Change each **mixed number** to an **improper fraction.** Show your work.

$1\frac{2}{4} = \dfrac{\boxed{6}}{\boxed{4}}$

$1 \times 4 = 4$

$4 + 2 = 6 \dashrightarrow \dfrac{6}{4}$

$5\frac{1}{3} = \dfrac{\square}{\square}$

$4\frac{5}{6} = \dfrac{\square}{\square}$

$3\frac{3}{4} = \dfrac{\square}{\square}$

$2\frac{1}{2} = \dfrac{\square}{\square}$

$4\frac{2}{7} = \dfrac{\square}{\square}$

$3\frac{5}{8} = \dfrac{\square}{\square}$

$6\frac{3}{5} = \dfrac{\square}{\square}$

$1\frac{5}{6} = \dfrac{\square}{\square}$

Changing mixed numbers to fractions

Fractions and Decimals

Brain Box

A **mixed number** is a whole number plus a fraction.

Example: $4\frac{2}{3}$

To change a mixed number to a fraction:

Step 1: Multiply the whole number by the denominator.

$4 \times 3 = 12$

Step 2: Add that number to the numerator.

$12 + 2 = 14$

Step 3: Write your answer above the denominator.

$\dfrac{14}{3}$

The resulting fraction is called an **improper fraction,** because the numerator is bigger than the denominator.

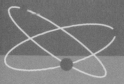

Change It Back

Change each **improper fraction** to a mixed number. Show your work.

$$\frac{7}{5} = \boxed{1} \ \frac{\boxed{2}}{\boxed{5}}$$

$$\begin{array}{r} 1 \ r \ 2 \\ 5\overline{)7} \\ -5 \\ \hline 2 \end{array}$$

$$\frac{7}{2} = \boxed{} \ \frac{\boxed{}}{\boxed{}}$$

$$\frac{7}{3} = \boxed{} \ \frac{\boxed{}}{\boxed{}}$$

$$\frac{8}{7} = \boxed{} \ \frac{\boxed{}}{\boxed{}}$$

$$\frac{18}{4} = \boxed{} \ \frac{\boxed{}}{\boxed{}}$$

$$\frac{14}{6} = \boxed{} \ \frac{\boxed{}}{\boxed{}}$$

$$\frac{10}{4} = \boxed{} \ \frac{\boxed{}}{\boxed{}}$$

$$\frac{15}{2} = \boxed{} \ \frac{\boxed{}}{\boxed{}}$$

$$\frac{11}{8} = \boxed{} \ \frac{\boxed{}}{\boxed{}}$$

Changing fractions to mixed numbers

Fractions and Decimals

Brain Box

An **improper fraction** can be changed to a mixed number.

Example: $\frac{15}{2}$

Step 1: Divide the numerator by the denominator.

$$\begin{array}{r} 7 \ r \ 1 \\ 2\overline{)15} \\ -14 \\ \hline 1 \end{array}$$

Step 2: The answer is the whole number. The remainder is the numerator. The denominator stays the same.

$$\frac{15}{2} = 7\frac{1}{2}$$

More or Less

Add or subtract these **mixed numbers.**

$8\frac{1}{3} + 5\frac{1}{3} = \boxed{}\,\frac{\boxed{}}{\boxed{}}$

$10\frac{1}{3} + 3\frac{1}{3} = \boxed{}\,\frac{\boxed{}}{\boxed{}}$

$6\frac{7}{8} - 4\frac{1}{8} = \boxed{}\,\frac{\boxed{}}{\boxed{}}$

$8\frac{1}{4} + 2\frac{2}{4} = \boxed{}\,\frac{\boxed{}}{\boxed{}}$

$9\frac{5}{7} - 4\frac{4}{7} = \boxed{}\,\frac{\boxed{}}{\boxed{}}$

$7\frac{6}{8} - 5\frac{5}{8} = \boxed{}\,\frac{\boxed{}}{\boxed{}}$

$7\frac{1}{5} + 2\frac{2}{5} = \boxed{}\,\frac{\boxed{}}{\boxed{}}$

$5\frac{9}{10} - 4\frac{1}{10} = \boxed{}\,\frac{\boxed{}}{\boxed{}}$

$6\frac{2}{4} + 8\frac{1}{4} = \boxed{}\,\frac{\boxed{}}{\boxed{}}$

$1\frac{1}{5} + 7\frac{2}{5} = \boxed{}\,\frac{\boxed{}}{\boxed{}}$

$3\frac{2}{8} + 1\frac{5}{8} = \boxed{}\,\frac{\boxed{}}{\boxed{}}$

$7\frac{8}{10} - 5\frac{3}{10} = \boxed{}\,\frac{\boxed{}}{\boxed{}}$

Adding and subtracting mixed numbers

Fractions and Decimals

Brain Box

To add mixed numbers: Example: $5\frac{3}{7} + 2\frac{1}{7} = 7\frac{4}{7}$

Step 1: Add the fractions.
$\frac{3}{7} + \frac{1}{7} = \frac{4}{7}$

Step 2: Add the whole numbers.
$5 + 2 = 7$

Step 3: Write out the mixed number.
$7\frac{4}{7}$

To subtract mixed numbers: Example: $6\frac{6}{9} - 4\frac{2}{9} = 2\frac{4}{9}$

Step 1: Subtract the fractions.
$\frac{6}{9} - \frac{2}{9} = \frac{4}{9}$

Step 2: Subtract the whole numbers.
$6 - 4 = 2$

Step 3: Write out the mixed number.
$2\frac{4}{9}$

Tenths Another Way

Write the **fraction** for each figure. Then write the equivalent **decimal**.

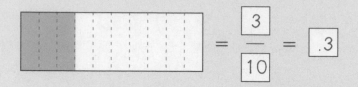 = $\dfrac{3}{10}$ = $.3$

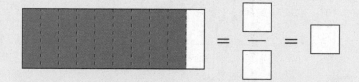 = $\dfrac{}{}$ = $\square$

 = $\dfrac{}{}$ = $\square$

$\dfrac{}{}$ = $\square$

Brain Box

A **decimal** is another way to write any fraction that has a denominator of 10, 100, 1,000, etc.

Example: $\dfrac{2}{10}$ = $.2$

decimal point   tenths

In decimals, the first digit to the right of the **decimal point** stands for **tenths.** Since this number is 2, we would say it is two-tenths.

$.2$ = **two-tenths** = $\dfrac{2}{10}$

Hundredths

Write the **fraction** for each figure. Then write the equivalent **decimal.**

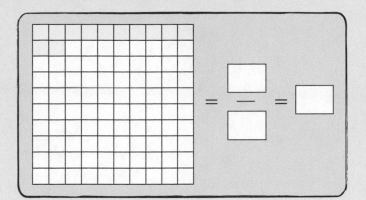 $= \dfrac{\boxed{}}{\boxed{}} = \boxed{}$

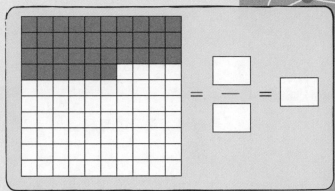 $= \dfrac{\boxed{}}{\boxed{}} = \boxed{}$

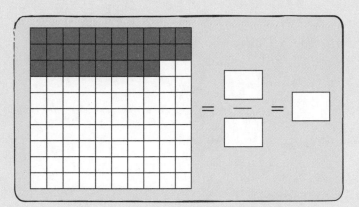 $= \dfrac{\boxed{}}{\boxed{}} = \boxed{}$

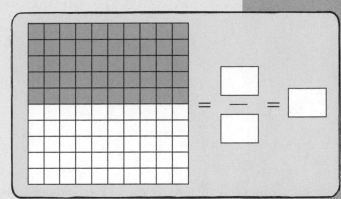 $= \dfrac{\boxed{}}{\boxed{}} = \boxed{}$

Write the **decimal** for each **fraction.**

$\dfrac{15}{100} = \boxed{}$ $\dfrac{43}{100} = \boxed{}$ $\dfrac{60}{100} = \boxed{}$

$\dfrac{30}{100} = \boxed{}$ $\dfrac{22}{100} = \boxed{}$ $\dfrac{7}{100} = \boxed{}$

$\dfrac{75}{100} = \boxed{}$ $\dfrac{19}{100} = \boxed{}$ $\dfrac{99}{100} = \boxed{}$

HINT:
The numerator
is less than 10!

Fractions and Decimals

Hundredths in decimals

Brain Box

The second digit to the right of the decimal point stands for **hundredths.**

Example: **.25** $= \dfrac{25}{100}$

tenths | hundredths

If there is less than 10 hundredths in a decimal, you write a 0 in the tenths column.

Example: **.01** $= \dfrac{1}{100}$

tenths | hundredths

Coins

Write the **decimal** for the coin described in each sentence.
Use a **dollar sign** to show that the amount stands for money.

The U.S. **penny,** or one-cent coin,
has been around since the 1790s. _$.01_

In 1864, the U.S. had a **2-cent piece.** _____

And in 1865, it had a **3-cent** coin. _____

The **nickel** has been around since the 1860s. _____

The **dime** is older than the nickel.
The dime goes back to the 1790s. _____

In 1875, the U.S. issued a **20-cent piece.** _____

The **quarter** goes back to the 1790s. _____

The **half-dollar** also goes back to the 1790s. _____

There is no such coin as a **75-cent piece.**
(If there were, it would be written as _____ .)

The **dollar** is 100 cents. _____

**Fractions and
Decimals**

Coins

Brain Box

Here is what U.S. coins look like in decimals:

$.01 $.05 $.10 $.25 $.50 $1.00

Round the Track

Add or subtract the **decimal numbers** below.

```
  1
 .27
+ .24
─────
 .51
```

```
 .71
+ .07
─────
```

```
 .95
− .07
─────
```

```
 .89
− .50
─────
```

```
 .18
+ .17
─────
```

```
 .29
− .18
─────
```

```
 .13
+ .09
─────
```

```
 3.09
+2.08
─────
```

```
 .43
− .41
─────
```

```
 .21
+ .36
─────
```

```
 8.30
+2.99
─────
```

```
 2.54
+1.22
─────
```

```
 6.95
+5.25
─────
```

```
 1.95
+3.67
─────
```

```
 .66
− .32
─────
```

Subtract the decimals.
Be sure to write the dollar sign in your answer.

```
 $7.25
−$6.92
──────
```

```
 $4.93
−$2.81
──────
```

```
 $5.27
−$4.50
──────
```

```
 $6.75
−$3.22
──────
```

```
 $10.50
−$2.25
──────
```

```
 $6.88
−$4.76
──────
```

```
 $7.54
−$1.55
──────
```

```
 $1.79
−$1.35
──────
```

Fractions and Decimals

Adding and subtracting decimals

Brain Box

To **add** or **subtract decimals**, be sure that the decimal points are lined up. Then add or subtract starting with the right-hand number. Carry the decimal point directly down into your answer.

Example:
```
  5.84
− 4.73
──────
  1.11
```

Down, Down, Down

Write the smallest decimal at the bottom of the page. Write the other decimals down along the side of the mountain in order from largest to smallest.

.50	.75	.99	.05	.30
.78	.49	.66	.21	.08

.99

Fractions and Decimals

Decimals in descending order

Brain Box

You can compare decimals by looking at the numbers in the tenths place. The higher the number, the larger the decimal. If two or more decimals have the same number in the tenths place, look at the number in the hundredths place. The higher the number, the larger the decimal.

Different but Equal

Write the **fraction** for each figure. Then write
the equivalent **decimal.**

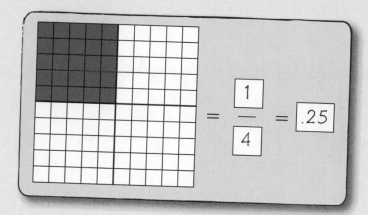

$= \dfrac{1}{4} = \boxed{.25}$

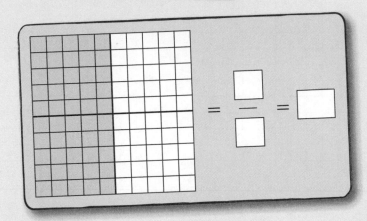

$= \dfrac{}{} = \boxed{}$

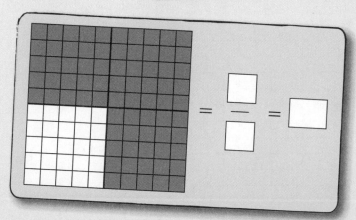

$= \dfrac{}{} = \boxed{}$

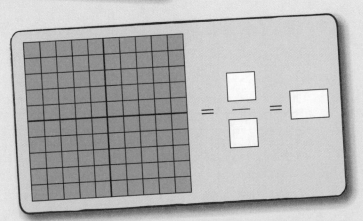

$= \dfrac{}{} = \boxed{}$

Big Time

Color each row of figures to show the **decimal** or **fraction**.
Then circle the bigger number in each row.

HINT: Since these grids are divided into one hundred squares, convert the fractions into hundredths to help you figure out how many squares to color.

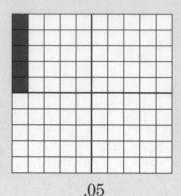

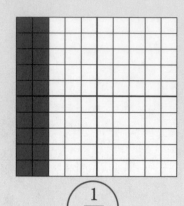

$$\frac{1}{5} \times \frac{20}{20} = \frac{20}{100} = .2$$

.05

$\left(\dfrac{1}{5}\right)$

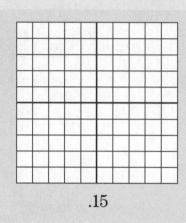

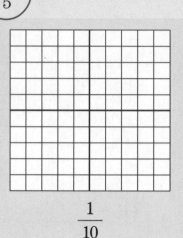

.15

$\dfrac{1}{10}$

Fractions and Decimals

Comparing fractions and decimals

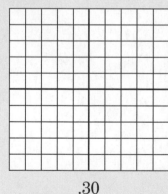

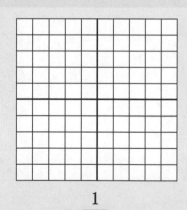

.30

$\dfrac{1}{2}$

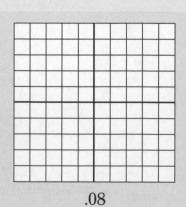

.08

$\dfrac{3}{4}$

More Money

Multiply. Be sure to write the dollar sign in your answers.

```
  11
$5.32          $1.50          $3.85          $4.00          $7.24
×   5          ×   8          ×   5          ×   7          ×   6
-----
$26.60
```

```
$3.89          $2.75          $9.95          $5.41          $7.00
×   2          ×   9          ×   4          ×   6          ×   5
```

```
$2.44          $6.05          $1.74          $8.25          $6.39
×  12          ×  10          ×  22          ×  50          ×  34
```

In 1891, a Seated Liberty half-dollar was worth $.50. Today, it's worth 300 times that. How much is it worth now? _____

Fractions and Decimals

Multiplying money

Brain Box

When you see a multiplication problem with a decimal, multiply as usual, ignoring the decimal point.

```
Example:   $3.57
           x    3
           -----
           1,071
```

When you're done, count how many digits are to the right of the original decimal.

```
$ 3 . 5 7
```

Put the decimal point into your answer the same number of digits in from the right.

```
$ 1 0 . 7 1
```

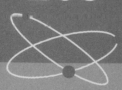

Less Money

Divide to find the quotient. Show your work.

```
    $1.43
3) $4.29
    3↓
    12↓
     9
    -9
     0
```

5) $5.00

6) $0.78

2) $15.00

7) $1.47

4) $7.60

2) $1.68

8) $0.88

5) $9.05

6) $4.26

Check the answer to the first problem by writing out a multiplication problem. Multiply the quotient by the divisor. Your answer should be the dividend.

```
    1
  $1.43
  ×  3
  $4.29
```

Fractions and Decimals

Dividing money

Suzanne, Raquel, and Orlando made $17.49 selling popcorn. They divided the money evenly. How much did each person get? _____

Brain Box

When you divide into a decimal, first put the decimal point in your answer. Keep the whole numbers to the left of the decimal point.

Example:
```
     .25
5) $1.25
```

Geometry and Measurement

Label the Lines

Label each **line segment** by its endpoints. Mark the shortest segment AB and the longest segment FG. Mark the other segment CD.

Draw two line segments. Name each segment by labeling both endpoints.

Draw two lines. Name each line by labeling two points on the line.

Parallel and perpendicular lines

Geometry and Measurement

Brain Box

A **line** goes in both directions and is named by any two points on the line. Points are usually labeled with letters, such as A, B, C, or D.

For example:

←•—•—→ = line AB or BA
  A B

A **line segment** is named by its two **endpoints.**
For example:

•————————• = line segment CD or DC
C   D

Along the Same Lines

Draw a circle around the sets that show **parallel** lines.

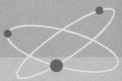

Brain Box

Parallel lines are lines that are the same distance apart at every point and can never meet or cross.

Perpendicular lines are lines that intersect at a 90° angle, which is called a **right angle.**

Geometry and Measurement

Parallel and perpendicular lines

Draw a circle around each set of **perpendicular** lines.

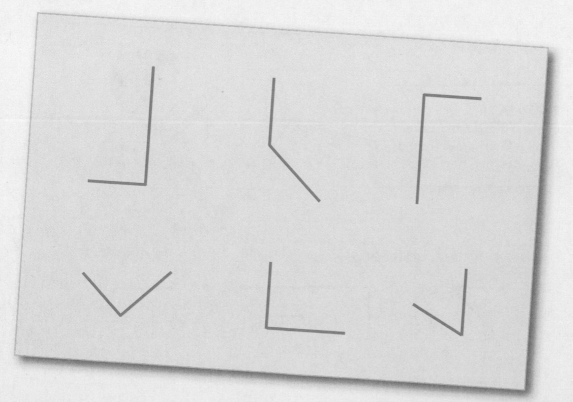

Many Sides

Write the number of sides below each **polygon.**

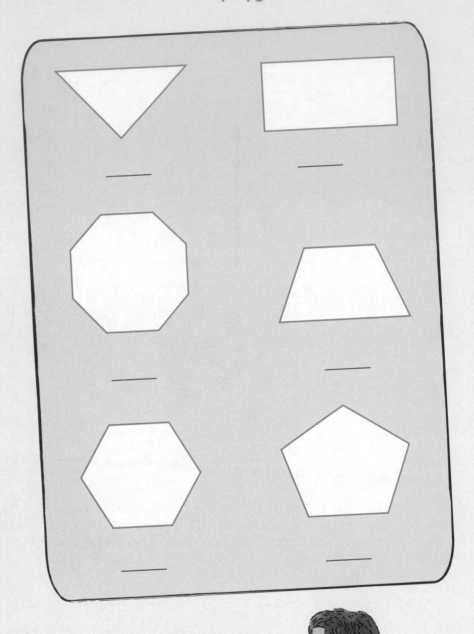

**Geometry and
Measurement**

Understanding
polygons and
angles

BRAIN FACT:
Poly is a prefix that means
"many." **Gon** comes from a
Latin word meaning "angle."

Write the name of each **angle.**

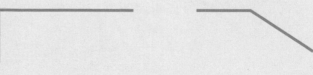

_____   _____   _____

Triangles

Circle each **isosceles** triangle.

Circle each **scalene** triangle.

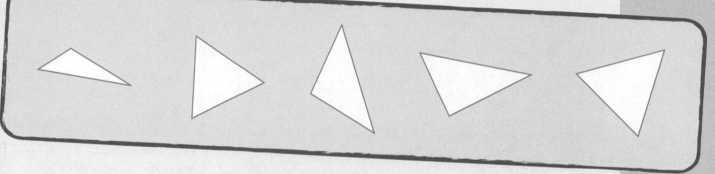

Circle each **equilateral** triangle.

Geometry and Measurement

Brain Box

A **triangle** is a closed figure with three straight sides.

In an **isosceles triangle,** two of the three sides are the same length.

In an **equilateral triangle,** all three sides are the same length.

In a **scalene triangle,** no three sides are the same length.

Every triangle has three angles. **Tri** is a prefix that means "three."

So Many Sides

Read about **polygons.** Then label each polygon.

A **polygon** is a closed figure with many angles and three or more straight sides. Polygons include:

- **Quad**rangle = 4 sides
- **Penta**gon = 5 sides
- **Hexa**gon = 6 sides
- **Hepta**gon = 7 sides
- **Octa**gon = 8 sides

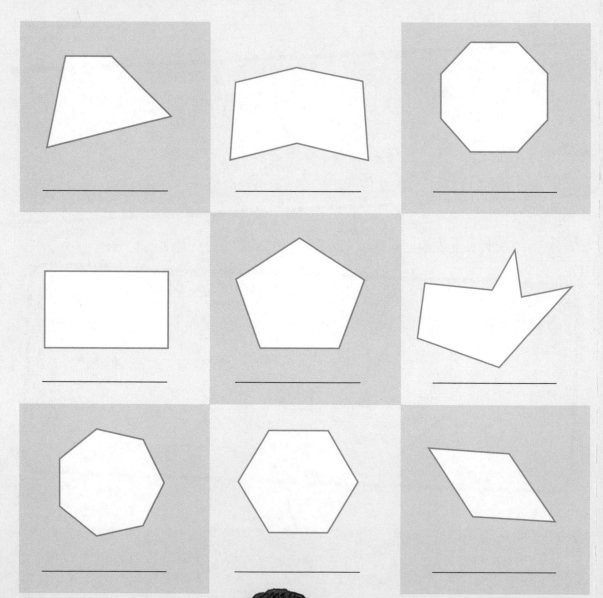

Geometry and Measurement

Polygons

BRAIN FACT:
A nine-sided polygon is called a **nonagon.**

Shape Up!

Read about **four-sided figures.** Then label each figure.

A **rectangle** is a four-sided figure that has four right angles.

A **square** is a rectangle with four equal sides.

A **quadrangle** (or **quadrilateral**) is a four-sided polygon that is not a rectangle.

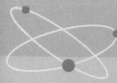

Meet the Circle

Read about **circles.**

A **circle** is a closed curved line on which every point is the same distance from the center.

The **radius** is a line segment from the center of the circle to any point on the edge.

The **diameter** is a line segment that passes through the center of the circle and whose ends touch the circle's edge.

Draw a **radius** on the circle from point A. Label the endpoint B. Then draw a diameter through the circle. Label it DE.

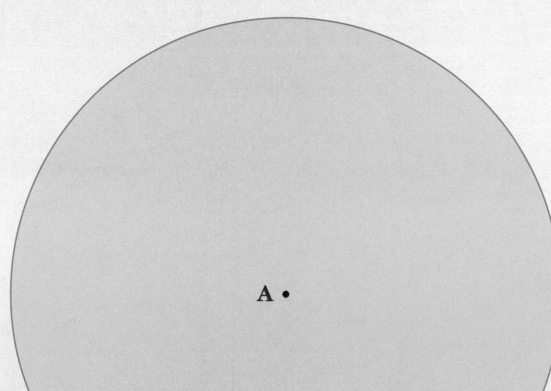

A •

Geometry and Measurement

Understanding circles

Through the Middle

Use the figure to answer the questions.

Name all the radii of this circle.

_____ _____ _____ _____

_____ is the diameter of this circle.

Which radius forms an acute angle with the diameter? _____

A diameter divides a circle in _____ .

Geometry and Measurement

Radius and diameter

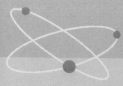

The Ruler

Cut out the ruler at the bottom of the page. Use it to measure the length in **inches** of each object. Be sure to include either abbreviation for the word inches in your answer.

Brain Box

An **inch** mark is written like this: "

The word **inch** is abbreviated like this: **in.**

You can use either one to indicate inches.

For example, you could write **3"** or **3 in.**

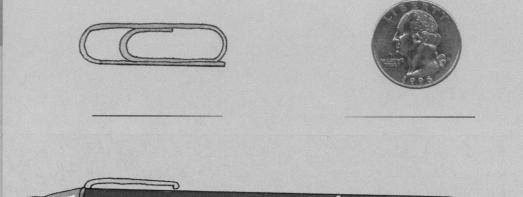

_____   _____

_____

_____

Using the ruler, draw a dot exactly two inches to the right of the red dot.

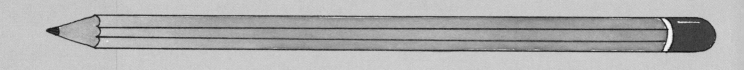

_____●_____

Draw a dot exactly 4" to the right of the green dot.

_____●_____

Measuring by inches

Geometry and Measurement

INCHES 1 2 3 4 5 6 7

CENTIMETERS
18 17 16 15 14 13 12 11 10 9 8 7 6 5 4 3 2 1

Brain Quest Fourth Grade Workbook

Going Metric

The bottom of the ruler you cut out is a **centimeter** ruler. Use it to measure the length of each item to the nearest centimeter. Be sure to include the abbreviation for the word centimeters in your answer.

BRAIN FACT:
The U.S.A., Liberia, and Burma are the only three countries in the world that don't use the metric system!

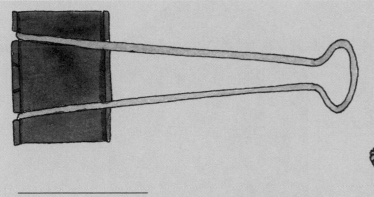

_____

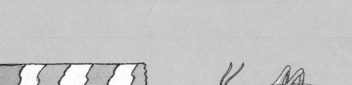

_____   _____   _____

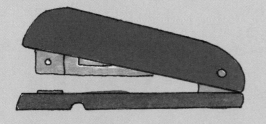

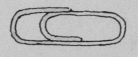

_____   _____

Measuring by centimeters

Geometry and Measurement

Measure the length of the flashlight. Write the length in inches and in centimeters.

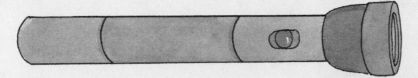

_____   _____

Brain Box

Centimeters, meters, and **kilometers** are the units of length in the metric system. The abbreviation for centimeters is **cm.** The abbreviation for meters is **m.**

Add the Sides

Write the **perimeter** below each polygon.

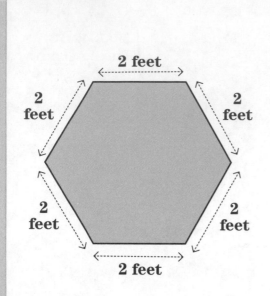

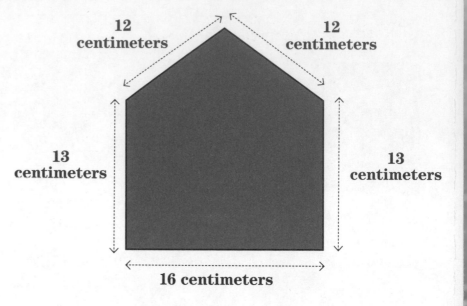

_____

_____

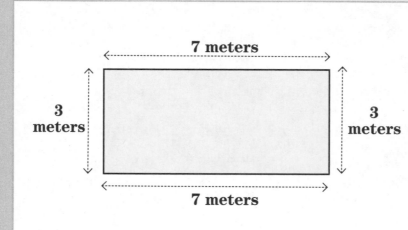

_____

_____

Brain Box

The **perimeter**
is the distance
around a figure.
You can find the
perimeter by
adding the lengths
of the sides.

2 + 2 + 2 + 2 = 8 **feet**

The perimeter of the
square is **8 ft.**

2 + 2 + 5 + 5 = 14 **centimeters**

The perimeter of the
rectangle is **14 cm.**

Length Times Width

Read about **area.** Then solve the problems.

The **area** of a figure is the number of square units inside a figure. You can find the area of a figure by using this simple formula:

Length × width = area

For example, this polygon is 5 inches long and 4 inches wide.

$5 \times 4 = 20$ square inches.

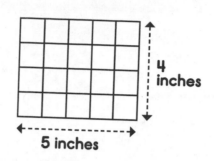

4 inches

5 inches

Find the **area** of each shape below. Be sure to write the correct abbreviation as part of your answer.

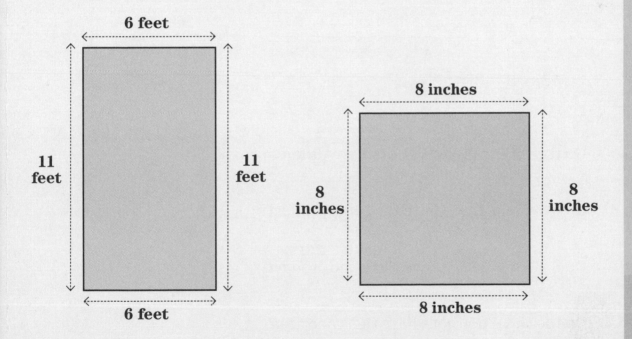

6 feet

11 feet   11 feet

6 feet

8 inches

8 inches   8 inches

8 inches

_____   _____

Finding area

Geometry and Measurement

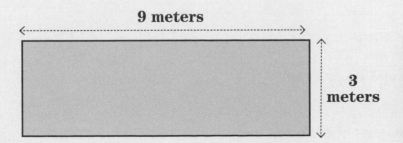

9 meters

3 meters

_____

Different Shape, Same Size

Find the **area** of each figure. Be sure to write the correct abbreviation as part of your answer.

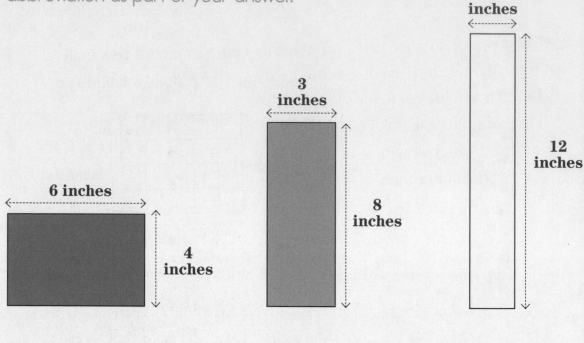

6 inches

4 inches

3 inches

8 inches

2 inches

12 inches

_____   _____   _____

Answer the questions.

Do the three polygons above have different shapes? _____

Do 6 × 4 and 12 × 2 have the same product? _____

Do 8 × 3 and 12 × 2 have the same product? _____

Do the three polygons have the same area? _____

List the factors of 24: ____ ____ ____ ____ ____ ____ ____ ____

If you drew a rectangle that was 24 inches long by 1 inch wide,

what would its area be? _____

Can polygons of different shapes have the same area? _____

Geometry and Measurement

Finding area

Three Dimensions

Read about **three-dimensional solids.**

Polygons are figures that have two dimensions: **length** and **width.** **Solids** are figures that have **three dimensions:** **length, width,** and **height.**

This figure has two dimensions: length and width

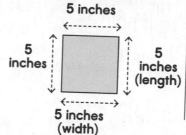

5 inches
5 inches
5 inches (length)
5 inches (width)

This figure has three dimensions: length, width, and height

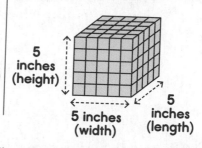

5 inches (height)
5 inches (width)
5 inches (length)

Write the length, width, and height of each figure.

length _____
width _____
height _____

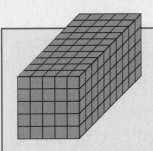

length _____
width _____
height _____

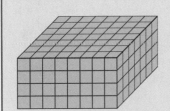

length _____
width _____
height _____

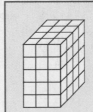

length _____
width _____
height _____

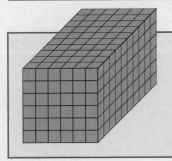

length _____
width _____
height _____

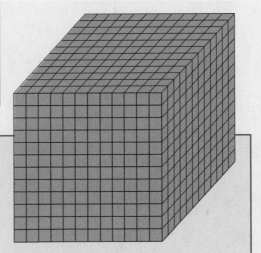

length _____
width _____
height _____

Geometry and Measurement

Understanding solid figures

What's Inside?

Read about **volume** and **cubic units**.

Volume tells you how many units will fit inside a solid.
These units are called **cubic units.**
You can find the volume of a solid figure by using this formula:
length × width × height = cubic units

Find the number of **cubic inches** in each figure.
Be sure to write the correct abbreviation as part of the answer.

Brain Box

Cubic units can be written as **cubic inches** or **cubic feet.**

Geometry and Measurement

Finding volume

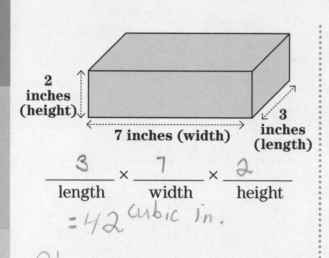

2 inches (height)

7 inches (width)

3 inches (length)

$$\underline{\quad 3 \quad} \times \underline{\quad 7 \quad} \times \underline{\quad 2 \quad}$$
length   width   height

= 42 cubic in.

21
$\times 2$
42

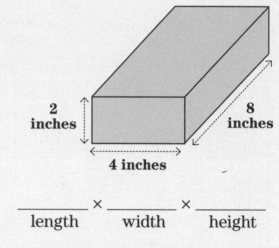

2 inches

8 inches

4 inches

$$\underline{\qquad} \times \underline{\qquad} \times \underline{\qquad}$$
length   width   height

= 64 cubic in.

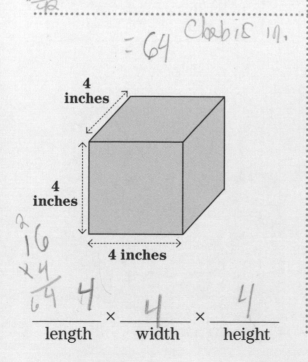

4 inches

4 inches

4 inches

2
16
$\times 4$
64

$$\underline{\quad 4 \quad} \times \underline{\quad 4 \quad} \times \underline{\quad 4 \quad}$$
length   width   height

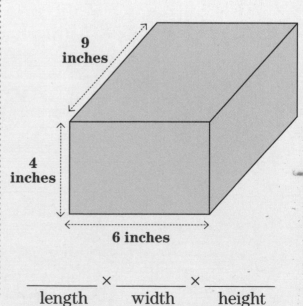

9 inches

4 inches

6 inches

$$\underline{\qquad} \times \underline{\qquad} \times \underline{\qquad}$$
length   width   height

From Cups to Gallons

Answer the questions about **liquid volume.** Show your work.

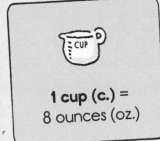

1 cup (c.) =
8 ounces (oz.)

1 pint (pt.) =
2 cups

1 quart =
2 pints

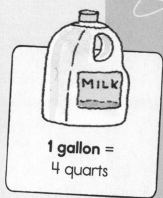

1 gallon =
4 quarts

Jackson drank one pint of milk for breakfast.

How many cups of milk did he drink? ___2___

Mr. Zonda starts his daylong hike with one gallon of water
divided into four equal containers.

How much does each container hold? ___1 quarts___

Elena's mother asked her to add a half-cup of water to the beans.

How many ounces of water did Elena add? ___?___

Mrs. Beverly brought two quarts of juice to class.

How many cups of juice could she pour for the students? _16 cups_

These containers are from smallest to largest.
Label each container using the measurements at the top of the page.

___pint___   ___pint___   ___quart___   ___gallons___

Ounces to Tons

Answer the questions about **weight.** Show your work.

1 pound (lb.) = 16 ounces (oz.)

1 ton = 2,000 pounds (lbs.)

How many ounces are there in 5 pounds? _____

How many pounds are there in 48 ounces? _____

Emily's backpack weighed 7 pounds and 3 ounces.

Joseph's backpack weighed 12 pounds and 15 ounces.

How much did the two backpacks weigh together? _____

Mouse the elephant weighs $2\frac{1}{2}$ tons.

How many pounds does he weigh? _____

Samuel's pumpkin weighed 17 pounds.

Butler's pumpkin weighed 13 pounds and 7 ounces.

How much more did Samuel's pumpkin weigh? _____

Geometry and Measurement

Weight measurements

Brain Box

Weight can be measured in **ounces** and **pounds.**

You can add, subtract, multiply, or divide pounds and ounces just as you would any other numbers. When you have pounds and ounces, you might have to change pounds into ounces before you can do the math.

Hot and Cold

Read about **temperature**.

Temperature is measured in units called **degrees**. The symbol for degrees is ° .
In the U.S., we measure temperature on a **Fahrenheit** thermometer.
Other countries measure temperature on a **Celsius** thermometer.

On the Fahrenheit scale:
- water freezes at 32°
- water boils at 212°
- normal body temperature is 98.6°

On the Celsius scale:
- water freezes at 0°
- water boils at 100°
- normal body temperature is 37°

Draw a blue line across both thermometers at their freezing point.

Draw a red line across both thermometers at their boiling point.

Draw a purple line across both thermometers at the normal body temperature point.

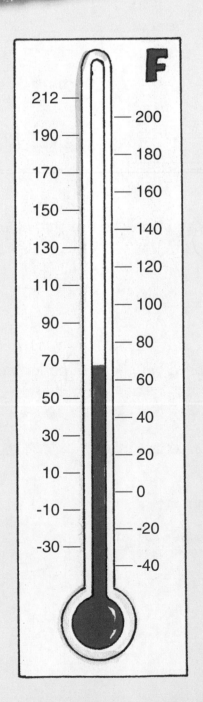

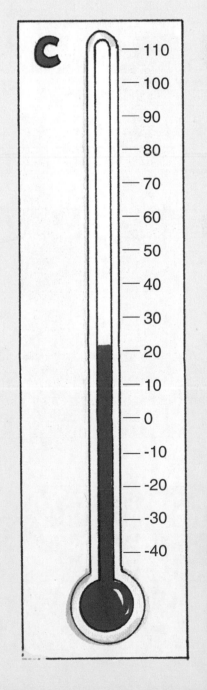

Geometry and Measurement

Temperature

Brain Box

Temperature is how hot or cold something is.

From Now to Then

Write the **time** on each line.

_____   _____   _____

Answer each question. Show your work.

How much time has gone by between the pink clock and the yellow clock?

_____

How much time has elapsed between the blue clock and the yellow clock?

_____

How much time has elapsed between the pink clock and the blue clock?

_____

Geometry and Measurement

Measuring time

Brain Box

To figure out how much time has gone by, or **elapsed,** subtract the way you would ordinary numbers.

For example:	7:45
	− 7:12
	0:33

33 minutes have elapsed between 7:45 and 7:12.

Probability and Data

What Are the Chances?

Use the picture to answer the questions about **probability**.

What are the chances of the hand landing on green? __1:6__

What are the chances of the hand landing on orange? _____

What are the chances of the hand landing on yellow? _____

Brain Box

Probability is the likelihood or chance that something will happen.

For example, a coin has two sides: heads and tails. If you toss a coin into the air and let it fall, the chances that it will come up heads are one in two. This probability is written as a ratio: **1:2**.

Use the picture to answer the questions.

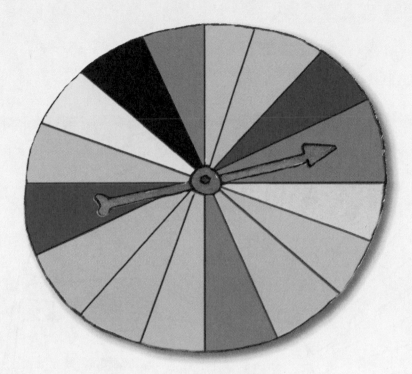

What are the chances of the hand landing on red? _____

What are the chances of the hand landing on orange? _____

What are the chances of the hand landing on black? _____

What are the chances of the hand landing on blue? _____

Probability

What are the chances of the hand landing on green? _____

**Probability
and Data**

What are the chances of the hand landing on yellow? _____

In the Cards

Use the picture to answer the questions.

If you separate all the red cards from a standard deck of cards, you will have 26 red cards.

What are your chances of drawing a diamond? _____

What are your chances of drawing a heart? _____

What are your chances of drawing a black card? _____

What are your chances of drawing a king? _____

What are your chances of drawing an ace of hearts? _____

Lift the Flap

Answer the following questions.

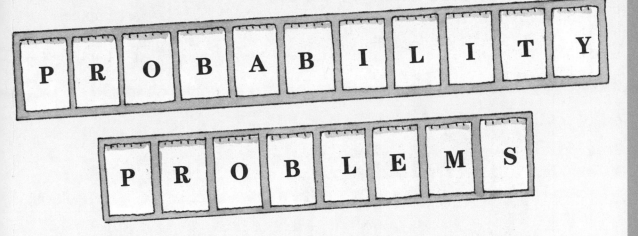

Suppose a prize worth $1,000 is hidden under the letters in
PROBABILITY.

What are the chances that it's hidden under the **O**? _____

What are the chances that it's hidden under the **B**? _____

What are the chances that it's hidden under an **I**? _____

Suppose the prize is hidden under the letters in **PROBLEMS.**
What are the chances that it's hidden under the **M**? _____

What is the probability that it's hidden under the **S**? _____

Now suppose that the prize is hidden under one of the letters of either
word. How many letters are there altogether? _____

What are the chances that the prize is hidden under a **P**? _____

What is the probability that it's hidden under a **B**? _____

What are the chances that it's hidden under a **T**? _____

Which letter has the highest probability of having the prize hidden
under it? _____

**Probability
and Data**

Probability

Puppies and Parakeets

Answer the questions using the **bar graph**.

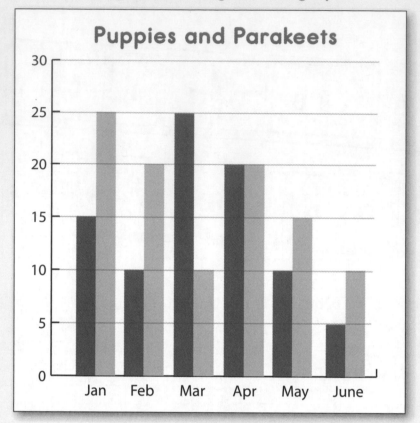

Puppies and Parakeets

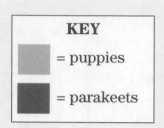

KEY
= puppies
= parakeets

This bar graph shows how many _____ and _____ were sold at Xeno's Pet Shop in half a year.

The half-year was from _____ to _____ .

What color bar is used to show puppy sales? _____

What was the largest number of puppies sold in any one month? _____

In what month were the most puppies sold? _____

What was the largest number of parakeets sold in any one month? _____

In what month were the most parakeets sold? _____

Which pet sold the least in any one month? _____

Which month was that? _____

In the half-year, a total of _____ puppies were sold and a total of _____ parakeets were sold.

Fund-Raising

Answer each question below using the **bar graph.**

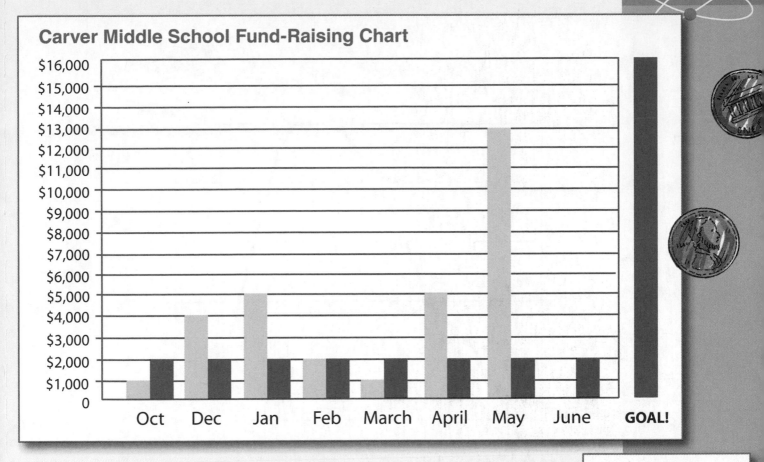

Carver Middle School Fund-Raising Chart

Carver Middle School wants to raise $16,000 for a science lab by June.
On what date did the fund drive start? _____

How much money has the school raised through May? _____

How much more money does the school need to raise in June to double
its goal?

_____

This graph shows that the school hoped to raise_____
every month for _____ months.

In what four months did the amount of money the school raised exceed
its monthly goal? _____

In what two months did the amount of money the school raised fall short
of its monthly goal? _____

In what month did the school raise more than six times
its monthly goal? _____

KEY

■ = goal

■ = actual money
raised

**Probability
and Data**

Understanding
graphs

Lost Gloves

The **line graph** shows the number of gloves turned in to the Lost and Found. Answer the following questions using the graph.

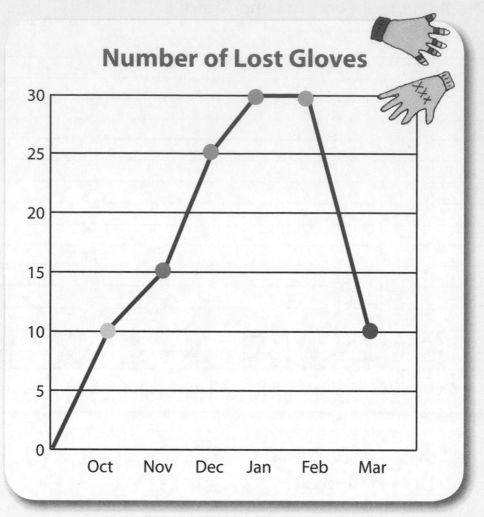

Number of Lost Gloves

This line graph shows the relationship between two things: the number of lost gloves and _____ .

How many gloves were turned in to the Lost and Found in October? ____

How many gloves were turned in in November? _____

As the weather got colder in December, were more or fewer lost gloves turned in to the Lost and Found than in November? _____

What happened in March, as the weather got warmer?

_____

Probability and Data

Line graphs

Brain Box

A **line graph** can be used to show how specific information changes over time.

Getting There

Answer the questions below by referring to the information shown in the following **pie chart.**

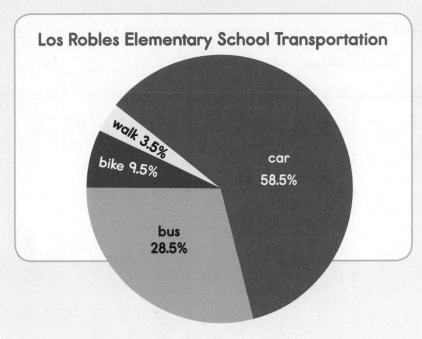

Los Robles Elementary School Transportation

walk 3.5%

bike 9.5%

car 58.5%

bus 28.5%

This pie chart gives data about how kids at the_____

_____ get to school every day.

The _____ section of the pie chart is the largest.
It represents transporation by _____.

The second largest section of the pie chart is _____.
It represents transportation by _____.

Almost 10% of kids _____ to school.

What percentage of students walk to school? _____

If the kids who take the bus to school biked instead, what percentage of the population would bike? _____

If 10% of the kids who drove in cars to school started walking instead, would the total numbers of kids who walked, rode bikes, or took the bus to school be greater than the number of kids who drove in cars? _____

Brain Box

A **pie chart** is a circle graph divided into sections, like a pie. Pie charts are an excellent way to show **parts** or **percentages** of the whole.

Probability and Data

Understanding pie charts

238

Homework vs. TV

Make your own **bar graph** comparing how much time you spend doing homework to how much time you spend watching TV.

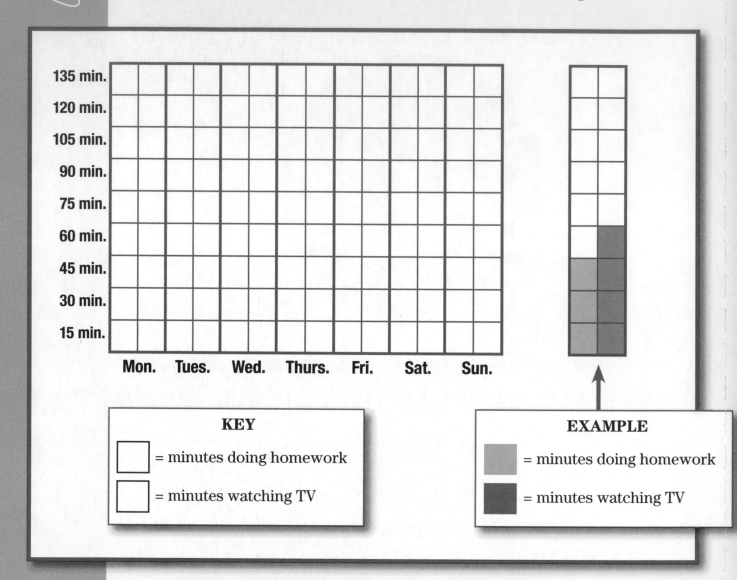

KEY

☐ = minutes doing homework

☐ = minutes watching TV

EXAMPLE

☐ = minutes doing homework

☐ = minutes watching TV

After you've finished the graph, answer the questions.

What is the total number of minutes you spent on homework? _____

Probability and Data

What is the total number of minutes you spent watching TV? _____

Line graphs

On what day did you watch the most TV? _____

On what day did you do the most homework? _____

Word Problems

Collecting Numbers

Solve the word problems. Use the extra space on the cards to show your work.

Ted and Truman held a contest to see who could collect more free baseball caps. Ted collected three caps in April, four in May, none in June, eight in July, three in August, and four in September. Truman collected one in April, seven in May, three in June, none in July, four in August, and three in September. How many caps did each boy collect?

Ted = _____ caps

Truman = _____ caps

What is the place value of the 2 in 124,683?

What is the difference between 75,238 and 118,500?

Write the digits 1 through 6 in reverse order to create a large number. Place a comma where it belongs. The number is:

How many zeros are there in five million?

Chloe makes extra money by baking brownies and selling them. At the end of one week, she earned $43.61. What was the average amount of money she earned every day that week?

Word Problems

Math skills

Number Games

Solve the word problems.

Logan plays number games with his pen pal in China.
One day, Logan wrote this sequence to his pen pal:

4   9   15   22

His pen pal wrote back the next three numbers.
What were they?

Rhonda is a bank teller who handled
$254,794 worth of money in a 10-hour
shift. Aiden, another teller, handled
$214,689. How much more money did
Rhonda handle than Aiden?

On Friday, Ethan sold
17 chocolate cookies
for $1.25 each. How
much money did he
make that day?

What is the sum of
234 and 87 rounded
to the nearest ten?

Subtract 55 from 188.
Then multiply by 3.
What number do you get?

Round 594,768 to the nearest ten thousand.

**Word
Problems**

Math skills

Skating Along

Solve the word problems.

What is the quotient of 472 divided by 8?

Using math symbols, write "Ten is less than fifteen."

The Smiths paid Maeve $6 an hour to babysit. The Blacks paid her $8 an hour. During one week, Maeve babysat for the Smiths for four hours and for the Blacks for three hours. How much did she earn that week?

What is the average of **14, 17, 90,** and **75?**

Subtract 700 from 1,532. Divide by 2. Multiply by 10.

Is it true that 15 < 10?

The Hometown Skates team was raising money for new hockey equipment. They needed to raise at least $1,000. A sponsor promised them that for every dollar they raised, he would donate two dollars. If the Hometown Skates raised $493, were they able to afford the new equipment?

Word Problems

Math skills

Bagging and Delivery

Solve the word problems.

The Boston Red Sox scored 48 runs in a three-game series. What was their average number of runs per game?

What is the product of 4,710 times 4?

Jack washed 128 cars in 8 hours. Approximately how many minutes did it take him to complete each car?

Subtract 23 minutes from 2 hours. What do you get?

Destiny bags 3 grocery bags a minute. How long will it take her to bag 150 bags?

Gabriel must divide 960 oranges into 80 gift baskets. How many oranges go into each basket?

Gabriel's boss tells him he must pack 12 boxes every quarter-hour. How many boxes must Gabriel pack in one hour?

Word Problems

Math skills

Roberto and his sister Elena go shopping at a farmer's market. Elena asks Roberto to buy $\frac{1}{4}$ pound of chives and $\frac{1}{2}$ pound of cilantro. How many ounces of chives should Roberto buy?

Philip pitched $1\frac{1}{3}$ innings on Monday and $3\frac{1}{3}$ innings on Wednesday. How many innings did he pitch in all?

Erika baked 7 pies and cut each pie into 7 pieces. She sold each piece for $1.65. At the end of the day, she had sold $\frac{3}{7}$ of a pie. How much did Erika earn that day?

Write these numbers in order from the smallest to the largest.

3.03   .30   0.03   3.30

Four friends worked together as dog walkers, sharing the profits. At the end of the month, they had earned a total of $1,179.36. How much did each friend make?

Morning Rush

Solve the word problems.

Every morning, Mr. Jackson takes the 7:03 train to work. It arrives at the downtown station at 7:57. How many minutes is Mr. Jackson on the train?

Mrs. Cohen takes the 6:42 train to work. It arrives at the downtown station at 7:57. How many minutes is Mrs. Cohen on the train? Write the answer as hours and minutes.

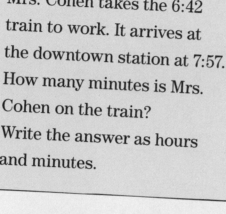

Write 7.3 as a mixed number.

Convert $\frac{2}{10}$ to a decimal.

Makayla mixes $\frac{5}{8}$ cup of syrup with $\frac{5}{8}$ cup of water and $\frac{7}{8}$ cup of juice. How many cups is the finished drink? Write the amount as a mixed number.

Word Problems

Math skills

Streets and Angles

Solve the word problems.

Hester ran $\frac{7}{8}$ of a mile on Monday, $\frac{9}{8}$ on Wednesday and $\frac{7}{8}$ on Friday. How far did she run that week? Write the answer as a mixed number.

What's the difference between 8.7 and 5.9?

Which line segment is $3\frac{1}{2}$ inches long?

A •————————————• B
C •—————————————• D
E •————————• F

Write the numbers 3, 4, and 5 as six different three-digit numbers.

When Jaime got to the corner, he realized that the street he was about to cross was perpendicular to the street that was next to him. This meant that the corner he was standing on was:

a. an acute angle

b. an obtuse angle

c. a right angle

Word Problems

Math skills

Brain Quest Fourth Grade Workbook

Perimeters

Answer the following word problems.

François draws a rectangle
that is 34 centimeters long by
21 centimeters wide. What is
the perimeter of the rectangle?

Every morning, Mia walks her Saint Bernard puppy
along the same oblong-shaped path. She walks 750 feet
in one direction and 1,325 feet in another direction.
Then she walks another 750 feet and another 1,325 feet.
What is the perimeter of the oblong that Mia walks?

Write the number of sides for each figure:

octagon _____

hexagon _____

pentagon _____

quadrangle _____

triangle _____

heptagon _____

If one side of
a square is 9
meters,
what is its
perimeter?

In one week, Drexel Dumpsters
collects 8,000 pounds of garbage.
How many tons of garbage is that?

Jasmine lives in an apartment
building that has 8 equal sides.
Each side is 8 yards. What is
the perimeter of the building?

**Word
Problems**

Math skills

Carpeted Area

Solve the word problems.

Maxie's room is 72 square feet. The carpeting she wants is sold by the square yard. Since nine square feet equals one square yard, how many square yards of carpeting does Maxie need?

Stefani wants to get new carpeting in her bedroom. Her bedroom is 9 feet by 10 feet. How many square feet is that?

The cost of the carpeting is $8.99 a square yard. Julio needs ten square yards. How much change will he get back if he pays with a $100 bill?

Kenji knows that the perimeter of a rectangle is 780 feet. He also knows that the length of the rectangle is 200 feet. What width does he give for the rectangle?

Tamar knows that the perimeter of a square is 384 centimeters. What is the length of one side of the square?

Preston is building a small box that is 55 centimeters by 35 centimeters. What is the area of the box?

Hiroko must pour cups of spring water into quart containers. She fills 17 quart containers. How many cups did she pour?

Social Studies

Seven Continents

Use the **map** in the back of this workbook to label the seven continents and the major oceans of the world.

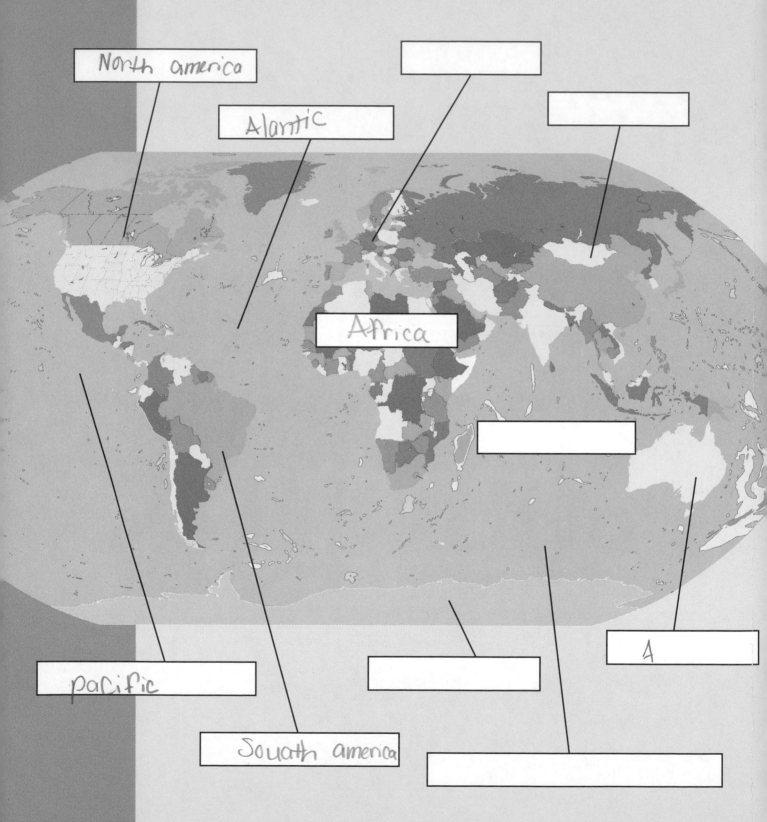

North america

Alantic

Africa

Pacific

Souath america

A

Earth Covers

Use the **map key** to complete each sentence.

The northern part of Africa is mainly _____ .

Which two continents have the most desert? _____

Antarctica is mostly _____ .

Does Asia have more grassland or mountains? _____

The three continents that have the largest mountain ranges
are _____ , _____ , and _____ .

Is there more land north of the equator or south
of the equator? _____

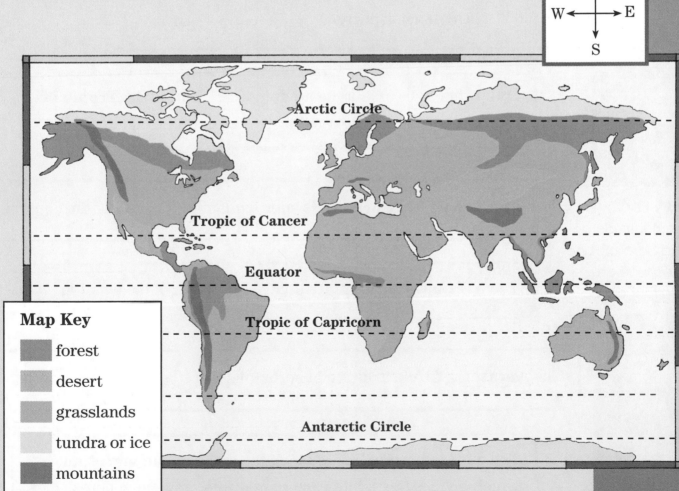

Map Key

■ forest
■ desert
■ grasslands
□ tundra or ice
■ mountains

Social Studies

Using a map
key

Imaginary Lines

Read about latitude and longitude.

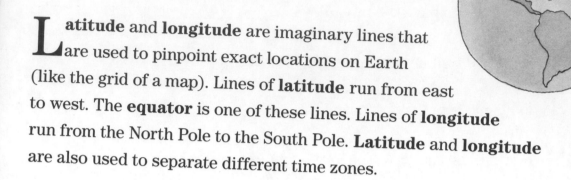

Latitude and **longitude** are imaginary lines that are used to pinpoint exact locations on Earth (like the grid of a map). Lines of **latitude** run from east to west. The **equator** is one of these lines. Lines of **longitude** run from the North Pole to the South Pole. **Latitude** and **longitude** are also used to separate different time zones.

The **equator** is an imaginary line of latitude around the center of the Earth. The **equator** divides Earth into a northern hemisphere and a southern hemisphere.

Four other lines of latitude are important. One is the **Tropic of Cancer,** which is approximately 23° north of the equator.

BRAIN FACT:
Lines of latitude are called parallels. Lines of longitude are called meridians.

The **Tropic of Capricorn** is approximately 23° south of the equator.

The **Arctic Circle** is approximately 66° north of the equator.

The **Antarctic Circle** is located approximately 66° south of the equator.

The most important line of longitude is the **prime meridian,** which divides Earth into eastern and western hemispheres.

Social Studies

Latitude and longitude

Label the map using the information on the previous page.

0° Longitude

66° north

23° north

0° Latitude

23° south

66° south

N
W ← → E
S

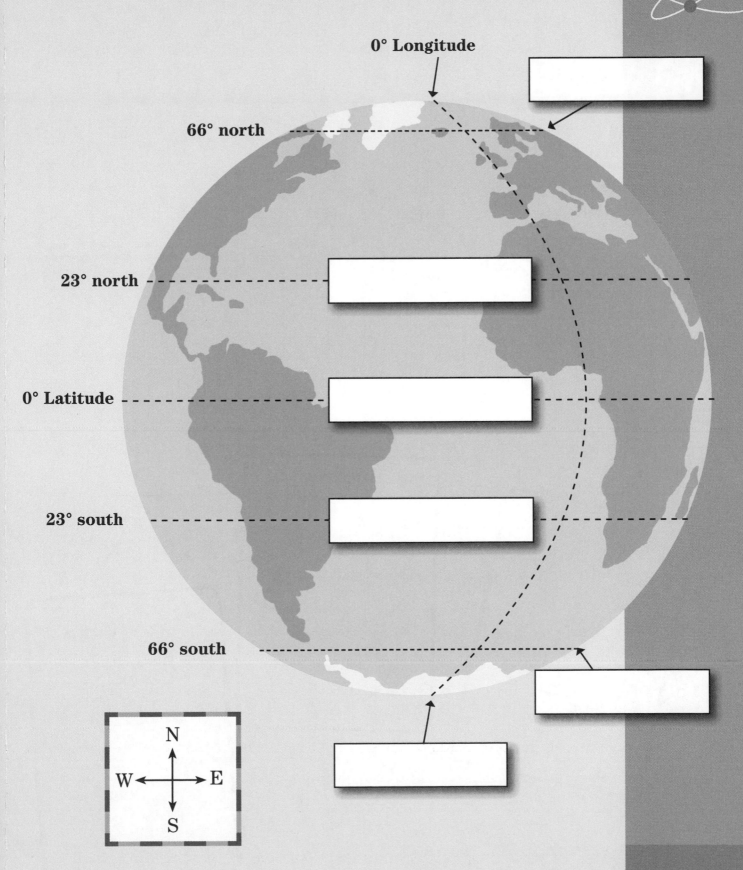

Social Studies

Latitude and longitude

Inventions and Creations

The **time line** shows inventions made between the years 1500 and 2000. Some of these have to do with the growing or storing of food. Some have to do with clothing, and some with communication. Write each invention or creation on the correct card including the year it was invented.

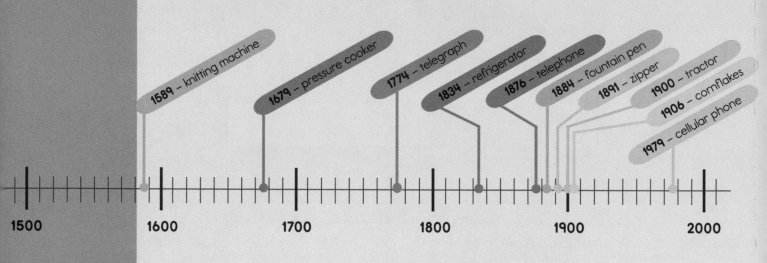

1589 – knitting machine
1679 – pressure cooker
1774 – telegraph
1834 – refrigerator
1876 – telephone
1884 – fountain pen
1891 – zipper
1900 – tractor
1906 – cornflakes
1979 – cellular phone

1500   1600   1700   1800   1900   2000

Food

Clothing

Communication

Reading
time lines

Brain Box

A **time line** shows the dates of specific events.

World Inventions

More inventions and discoveries are listed below. Write each one on the time line. Use blue pen for transportation and red pen for science.

Science

1590 – compound microscope
1796 – smallpox vaccination
1880 – seismograph
1928 – penicillin
1969 – artificial heart
1986 – synthetic skin

Transportation

1620 – submarine
1775 – steamship
1835 – propeller
1861 – bicycle
1885 – automobile
1937 – jet engine

1500   1600   1700   1800   1900   2000

What do you think were the three most important inventions of the last 500 years? Why?

Social Studies

Making a time line

The Thirteen Colonies

Read about the original thirteen colonies. Use the map to answer the questions.

What was the southernmost colony? _____

The colonies were situated along the eastern seacoast. What ocean did they border? _____

Which very large colony was north of Pennsylvania? _____

Which small colony is west of Rhode Island and east of New York? _____

Which colony is north of North Carolina? _____

The Original Thirteen Colonies

In 1607, the first wave of settlers left England for North America. They settled in an encampment in Virginia they called Jamestown, in honor of England's King James I.

The pilgrims followed soon after. They arrived on a ship called the Mayflower, and called their settlement "New" England.

Over the next hundred years, waves of settlers arrived and established settlements in what became known as the original thirteen colonies.

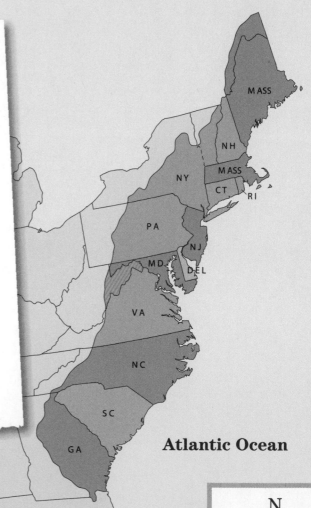

Atlantic Ocean

Gulf of Mexico

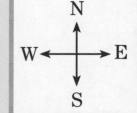

July 4, 1776

Read about the Declaration of Independence.

Many people in the American colonies believed they were being treated unjustly by the king of England. On July 4, 1776, representatives of these colonies met to sign a document. In it, they listed their reasons for separating from Great Britain to create a brand-new nation: The United States of America. This document was the Declaration of Independence.

Draw a line to match each pink card quoting the Declaration of Independence to the blue card explaining it.

King George of England "has kept among us, in times of peace, Standing Armies without the Consent of our legislatures."

The colonists wanted to sell their grains and furs and fish to other countries, but King George would not let them.

King George is "quartering large bodies of armed troops among us."

Colonial families were forced to have one or more British soldiers live with them and eat their food.

King George is "cutting off our Trade with all parts of the world."

The colonists were forced to pay taxes but were not allowed to vote on whether or not they wanted the taxes.

King George is "imposing Taxes on us without our Consent."

The colonists had not given their permission to have the British army stationed all over the colonies.

Social Studies

Reading an original document

Heading West

The Oregon Trail

During the 1840s, 1850s, and 1860s, tens of thousands of American families headed west. They followed a string of natural landmarks that became known as the Oregon Trail, a 2,000-mile path between Missouri and Oregon. The journey was dangerous, and the pioneers endured many hardships in their quest to reach California or the Oregon Territory.

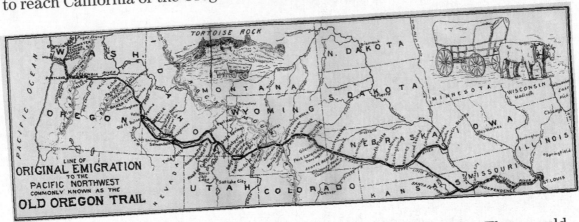

Families often used covered wagons to make the journey west. They would load up as many supplies as they could inside the wagons. Because there was seldom any room left, most people walked on foot the whole way.

It often took up to six months to make the journey. Though some people headed west for the gold, most went in search of farmland. The government was giving away land in an effort to get people to colonize the western territories.

There were many perils on the trail. River crossings were especially dangerous. The wagons themselves offered little protection against thunderstorms. And if the journey took too long, there was the danger of getting caught on the trail during winter. This is what happened to the Donner party in 1846 as they were making their way through the Sierra Mountains. The trail was blocked by snow and they were forced to wait out the winter on the near side of the mountain. Of the 81 people who started on that journey, only 45 survived the winter.

Answer the questions about the Oregon Trail.

Why did people want to head west?

_____

_____

_____

_____

Where did the Oregon Trail start? _____

How long was the Oregon Trail? _____

What were some of the perils the pioneers faced
as they headed west?

_____

_____

_____

_____

If you and your family had lived in the 1840s, do you think you would
have made the journey out west? Why or why not?

_____

_____

_____

_____

Social Studies

The Oregon
Trail

Counting the People

Read about the **census**.

In 1790, soon after the new government of the United States was formed, it established that a **census** would be taken every 10 years. A census is an official counting of the people in a country. A census also collects information about the people, such as their age, gender, race, religion, job, and so on.

	1790	1890	1990
Georgia	82,548	1,837,353	6,478,126
Massachusetts	378,787	2,238,943	6,016,425
New York	340,120	5,997,853	17,990,455
Pennsylvania	434,373	5,258,014	11,881,643
All States Total	3,893,035	62,116,811	248,709,873

Fill in the blanks with the correct year or state.

In _____, New York had fewer people than Pennsylvania did.

By _____, New York had more people than Pennsylvania did.

In 1790, the least populated of these four states was _____.

By 1890, _____ and _____ each had more people than the total population of the United States in 1790.

By 1890, the least populated of these four states was _____.

By 1990, the least populated of these four states was _____.

By 1990, each of the four states had more people than the total population of the United States in _____.

Imagine that you're a census taker. What information would you want to find out about people? Write four questions that you would ask.

1.

2.

3.

4.

Your State

Study the map of the United States.

HINT: If you need help answering these questions, look in an atlas or an encyclopedia for more information about the United States.

Answer the questions.

What is the name of your state? _____

Write the names of the states that border your state.

_____

_____

There is one place in the United States where four states meet.
They are called the four corner states. Can you name them?

_____ _____ _____ _____

What state is a chain of islands? _____

What state is farthest east on the U.S. mainland? _____

Go Online

Research your state in an atlas, an encyclopedia, or on the Internet. Fill in as much information as you can on the lines below.

State name: _____

Joined the Union on: _____

State nickname: _____

Capital city: _____

State flower: _____

State tree: _____

State bird: _____

State mammal: _____

State insect: _____

State rock: _____

If your state has had a centennial celebration (100th anniversary of statehood), when was it? _____

If it hasn't yet, when will it be? _____

If your state has had a bicentennial celebration (200th anniversary of statehood), when was it? _____

If it hasn't, when will it be? _____

Social Studies

State facts

Design Your Own

Imagine that your state has asked young people to design a new state flag. Create your own design, incorporating state symbols such as the state flower and state bird, as well as your favorite landmark or any other symbols. Draw your new flag below.

State Events

Use one library source and one online source to learn about important events in the history of your state. Choose one of these events to learn more about.

Use the **idea web** below to organize your research. Write the state event in the center circle and fill each smaller circle with a detail about the event. You might want to research things like the date the event happened, key historical figures involved, the exact location of the event, and so on.

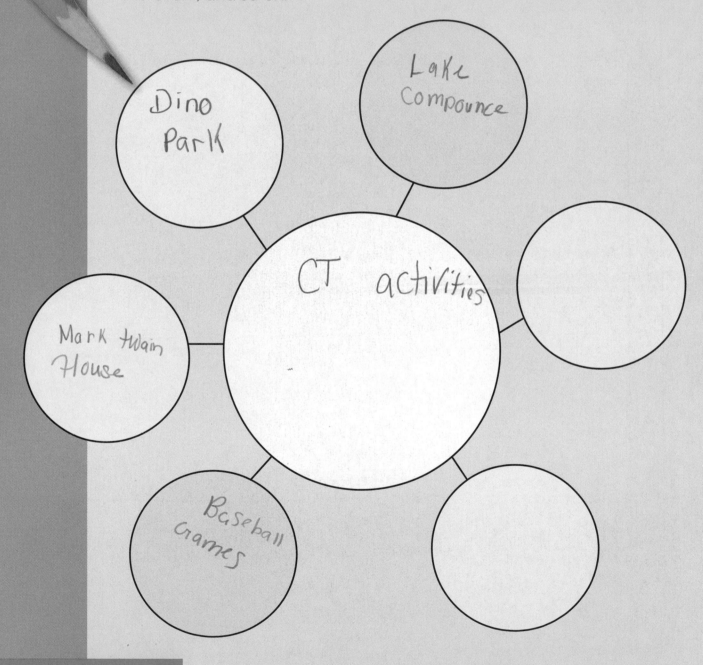

Dino Park

Lake Compounce

Mark twain House

CT activities

Baseball Games

Brain Box

You can organize your research by making an **idea web.**

Refer to your idea web on the previous page and use your notes to write an outline for a three-paragraph report about the state event you researched. Make each paragraph about a different topic, and fill in the supporting details you'll use in your writing.

Paragraph 1 topic _____

   Supporting detail _____

   Supporting detail _____

   Supporting detail _____

Paragraph 2 topic _____

   Supporting detail _____

   Supporting detail _____

   Supporting detail _____

Paragraph 3 topic _____

   Supporting detail _____

   Supporting detail _____

   Supporting detail _____

Social Studies

Write an outline

Report It

Now it's time to write! Write your three-paragraph report using the outline you made on the previous page. Be sure to include a topic sentence in each paragraph.

Science

The Universe

Read about the **universe** and **galaxies**.

The Big Picture

Everything that exists—our world, our sun, our galaxy, all of outer space and even time—lives within the universe. Scientists believe that the universe began with a huge explosion, the Big Bang, somewhere between 10 and 20 billion years ago. Out of that explosion the stars and galaxies and planets came into being.

There are hundreds of billions of galaxies in the universe. There are hundreds of billions of stars in every galaxy. There are also other celestial bodies like planets, asteroids, comets, satellites, black holes, clouds of cosmic dust and gas called nebulae, and what scientists call "dark matter," which is all the stuff we cannot see.

There are three types of galaxies: spiral, elliptical, and irregular. Our solar system is part of the Milky Way galaxy, which is a spiral galaxy.

BRAIN FACT: Another word for universe is cosmos, which means "order." The universe is bound by gravity, which brings order to the way the universe functions.

Name at least five types of celestial bodies in the universe.

_____

_____

_____

Name the three types of galaxies.

_____

_____

Scientists believe that the universe began with an
explosion billions of years ago. This is called the

_____ theory.

What are nebulae? _____

What do scientists call the stuff in the universe we can't see?

_____

What is the name of our galaxy? _____

What is another word for universe? _____

The universe

Science

The Solar System

Read about the **solar system.** Then read about the planets on the following page.

A Tour of Our Solar System

Our solar system is made up of the sun, which is at the very center of our system, and the eight planets—plus dwarf planets, asteroids, and meteors—that orbit the sun.

The eight planets that orbit the sun are: Mercury, Venus, Earth, Mars, Jupiter, Saturn, Uranus, and Neptune. A good way to remember the order of the planets is to remember this sentence: **M**y **V**ery **E**ducated **M**other **J**ust **S**howed **U**s **N**everland.

Answer the questions about the planets.

What planet looks blue because of its methane gas? _____

What planet orbits the sun in 88 days? _____

Which is the largest planet in the solar system? _____

What dwarf planet is no longer considered to be a major planet in our solar system? _____

What planet is known as the red planet? _____

What major planet is covered in an icy layer of clouds? _____

What planet is third from the sun? _____

What planet is known for its beautiful rings? _____

Which planet is the hottest? _____

Earth, our home planet, is the third planet from the sun. It takes 365 days to orbit the sun.

Earth has one moon.

Pluto used to be considered a planet, but is now called a dwarf planet. It takes Pluto 247.7 Earth years to orbit the sun. That means a plutonian year is 90,410 days long!

Pluto has three moons.

Saturn is known for its beautiful rings, which are chunks of ice and rocks as small as the head of a pin or as large as an elephant. It takes Saturn 29.5 Earth years to orbit the sun.

Saturn has 31 moons.

The last major planet in the solar system is **Neptune.** The blue color of Neptune is due to methane gas in its atmosphere, which absorbs all the red light. There is a constant storm raging over Neptune, with winds blowing ten times faster than the worst hurricanes on Earth. It takes almost 165 Earth years for Neptune to orbit the sun.

Neptune has eight moons.

Uranus is a frozen planet completely covered in an icy layer of clouds. It takes Uranus 84 Earth years to orbit the sun.

Uranus has 27 moons.

Venus, the second planet from the sun, is covered in a thick layer of clouds. These clouds are made of sulfuric acid, which trap the heat of the sun on the surface of Venus and makes it our solar system's hottest planet.

Jupiter is the fifth planet from the sun and the largest planet in the solar system. It is 318 times the size of Earth, and is made up of gases that give it a red and orange glow. A great red spot in the center of Jupiter is a giant cloud swirling in the opposite direction of all the other clouds. It takes Jupiter 11.86 Earth years to orbit the sun.

Jupiter has 63 moons!

Mercury, the planet closest to the sun, looks a lot like our moon. It is covered in craters, and it has no atmosphere. It takes Mercury 88 Earth days to orbit the sun.

Mars, the fourth planet from the sun, is known as the red planet because of its desertlike landscape. It has long grooves in the land from rivers that flowed there 4 billion years ago. There might have once been life on Mars, though the atmosphere is too thin to support life now. It takes Mars 686.98 Earth days to orbit the sun.

Mars has two moons.

Courtesy of NASA/JPL

The Moon

Read about the moon.

It takes the moon 27 days and 7 hours to go around Earth once. As it orbits around Earth, the moon is illuminated by the sun in different ways, depending how the sun, Earth, and moon line up. Each of the different "looks" of the moon is called a lunar phase.

SUNLIGHT

Last Quarter (Half Moon)

Waning Crescent

Waning Gibbous

New Moon

Full Moon

Waxing Crescent

First Quarter (Half Moon)

Waxing Gibbous

Use the diagram to answer the questions.

When the moon is between the sun and the Earth, it is completely in the shadows. This lunar phase is called a _____.

A _____ appears as a complete circle in the night sky.

There are two times in a lunar cycle when we only see a sliver of the moon. These are called the _____ and _____ phase.

Another term for a last quarter moon and a first quarter moon is a _____ moon.

How long does it take the moon to orbit Earth? _____

Where do you think the word "month" comes from? _____

A gibbous moon is when more than half the moon is visible.
A _____ comes before the full moon phase. A _____ comes after a full moon phase.

BRAIN FACT:
"Waxing" means growing.
"Waning" means shrinking.

The Earth

Read about our home planet.

The Earth is the only planet we know of, so far, on which there is life. At 7,926 miles in diameter, the Earth is the fifth largest planet in our solar system. It is 93 million miles from the sun, and 4.6 billion years old. Scientists know this because they have studied rocks to determine how old they are.

The Earth, like all the planets in our solar system, orbits the sun. It takes the Earth 365.26 days to do this, which is how we measure an Earth year. While the Earth is orbiting, it is also spinning on its axis. It takes 24 hours for the Earth to make one rotation around its axis. This is an Earth day.

The Earth's axis is tilted, so different parts of the planet face the sun at different times of the year. This is why we have four seasons: summer, autumn, winter, and spring.

There is a thin layer of gases that surrounds the Earth. This is called the Earth's atmosphere. The Earth's atmosphere has changed over millions of years. It has allowed life on Earth to grow, and to evolve.

Answer the questions.

How big is the planet Earth? _____

How did scientists determine that the Earth is 4.6 billion years old?
_____

What is the thin layer of gas that surrounds the Earth? _____

How long does it take the Earth to rotate on its axis? _____

How far is the Earth from the sun? _____

BRAIN FACT:
Even though the Earth is huge, it's tiny compared to the sun. One million Earths could fit inside the sun!

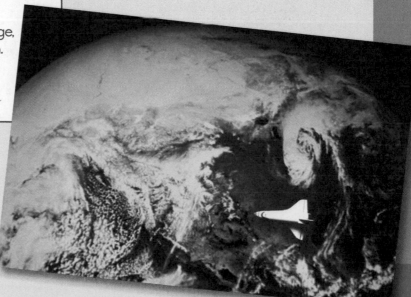

Earth

Science

Shapers of the Earth

Use the pictures to label the cards with a word from the Word Box.

hurricane ✓	volcano ✓	earthquake ✓	glacier ✓	flood ✓	wind

hurricane

This powerful ocean storm causes great damage when it hits land. Katrina, for example, washed away Louisiana beaches and submerged some islands.

Flood

This is an overflowing of water outside its normal boundaries. It can uproot trees, wash away topsoil, and wipe out towns.

earthquake

This force causes the earth to move suddenly and violently along fault lines. In 1812, the Mississippi River's course was changed by one of these.

Wind

Unlike some natural forces that cause immediate changes in the earth's surface, this force works over time. It can carve rocks into strange shapes.

Grtaejer

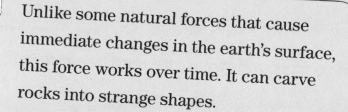

This huge sheet of ice scrapes basins into the earth and creates lakes. The Great Lakes were formed by this force.

Volcanc

When this erupts, lava is sent into the air and down its sides. In the ocean, one of these can form an island or island chain, such as Hawaii.

Brain Box

Land-forms can be shaped by natural forces such as volcanic activity, earthquakes, and wind.

Earthquakes, volcanoes, and others

Science

Rocks and Minerals

Read about **rocks and minerals.** Then answer each question with a word from the Word Box.

A **mineral** is a substance whose physical properties are the same throughout.

A **rock** is an aggregate (combination) of minerals. A rock might not have the same physical properties throughout.

lava	granite	copper	shale	talc	graphite

This mineral was used to make tools 10,000 years ago because it can be hammered into shape. It conducts electricity well, and you probably have some of it in your piggy bank in the form of pennies. _____

When a volcano erupts, you'll see this very hot and liquid igneous rock.

_____

This is one of the softest of all minerals. It can be ground up and made into a body powder or talcum powder. It is called _____ .

_____ is the most common sedimentary rock, formed from mud or clay. You can see the layers in this rock, and sometimes they break off easily. This rock is used to make bricks and cement.

This soft metamorphic rock is used to make lead pencils. It is slippery and can be used to lubricate machinery. This rock is called _____ .

This igneous rock is very common on Earth. It is made of quartz, feldspar and mica, and you can see the crystals in the rock. This rock, called _____, is often used for kitchen countertops.

Knowing rocks and minerals

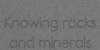

Science

Everything's Related

Read about **solids**, **liquids**, and **gas**.

Why Matter Matters

Everything in the universe is made up of either **matter** or **energy**. Matter is everything that takes up space. It is made up of tiny particles called atoms and molecules that are so small they can only be seen with powerful microscopes. No matter how big or small, matter has mass—it can be weighed even if it's as light as a feather.

Matter has three common states:

Solid

A solid has a hard or firm surface. It has a fixed volume. It can hold its shape.

Liquid

A liquid is fluid and can flow freely. It will take the shape of whatever contains it.

Gas

A gas has no shape or volume. It will expand indefinitely.

Sometimes the state of matter is determined by temperature. For instance, water is a liquid. When water is frozen it becomes ice, which is a solid. When water is boiled it becomes steam, which is a gas.

Identify each state of matter by writing either **solid, liquid,** or **gas** next to it.

a desk _____   an icicle _____

mist _____   milk _____

maple syrup _____   helium in a balloon _____

It's All Relative

Energy is everything in the universe that is not matter. It's not a solid, a liquid, or a gas—and it's everywhere around us. It's what gets everything in the universe going. Heat, light, sound, and motion are all different forms of energy. Energy can change forms, but it can never be made and it can never be ended. In fact, the most important scientific principle is called *the Law of the Conservation of Energy*, which states that energy can neither be created nor destroyed, but it can be transformed from one form to another.

Energy can be converted into matter and matter can be converted into energy. For instance, although we can't see it, we know there is a core of matter at the very center of the sun. That fiery glow that surrounds the sun is caused by that core of matter being converted into energy. This is what causes all stars to shine.

It was Albert Einstein who, in 1905, first theorized that all matter contained the possibility of being converted into energy. In fact, the tiniest amounts of mass could actually be converted into huge amounts of energy. He came up with an equation that could be used to figure out how much energy any amount of matter might actually contain.

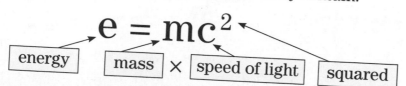

$$e = mc^2$$

| energy | mass | × | speed of light | squared |

His theory on the relationship between matter and energy revolutionized the way scientists viewed the universe. Much of what we know about how the universe works today is due to the work of Albert Einstein.

What does *the Law of the Conservation of Energy* state?

_____

What causes the sun to glow? _____

_____

When did Einstein write his theory about matter and energy? _____

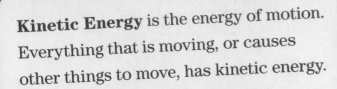

Kinetic and Potential

Read about the two types of **energy.** Then answer the questions.

Kinetic Energy is the energy of motion. Everything that is moving, or causes other things to move, has kinetic energy.

Examples of **kinetic energy:**

- electricity, because electrical charges cause things to move

- magnets, because magnetic forces cause things to move

- light, heat, solar, and wind energy, because these energies cause things to move

- sound, since sound is caused by vibrations that are carried on sound waves

Potential Energy is energy that can be put into motion. It is energy that is stored and waiting to happen.

Examples of **potential energy:**

- gasoline, propane, and petroleum (chemical energy)

- coils and springs that have been compressed, rubber bands that have been stretched (mechanical energy)

- the energy stored inside an atom (nuclear energy)

- a boulder at the top of a hill, since it could be pushed off the hill and roll downward (gravitational energy)

Write **K** next to the things that have **kinetic energy.**
Write **P** next to the things that have **potential energy.**

An apple hanging from a tree _____

An apple falling from a tree _____

A bolt of lightning _____

A moving windmill _____

Gasoline _____

Kinetic energy is the energy of _____

A rubber band that is stretched—but has not been released—is an

example of _____ energy.

Once the rubber band has been released and goes flying through the air,

its energy turns into _____ energy. Why does this happen?

_____

Why is sound considered a type of kinetic energy?

_____

Name three other examples of kinetic energy.

_____

_____

_____

Name three examples of potential energy.

_____

_____

_____

Why kind of potential energy is stored inside an atom?

_____

Root to Flower

Read about the different **parts of a plant.**
Label each card with a word from the Word Box.

seeds	root	bud	flower	fruit	leaf	stem

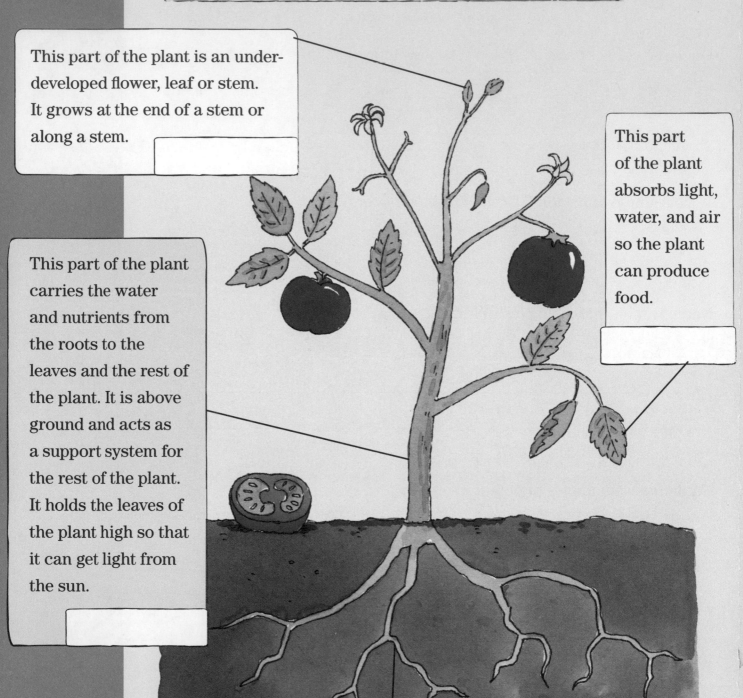

This part of the plant is an under-developed flower, leaf or stem. It grows at the end of a stem or along a stem.

This part of the plant absorbs light, water, and air so the plant can produce food.

This part of the plant carries the water and nutrients from the roots to the leaves and the rest of the plant. It is above ground and acts as a support system for the rest of the plant. It holds the leaves of the plant high so that it can get light from the sun.

This part of the plant absorbs nutrients and water through the soil to feed the rest of the plant. It can also store food that the plant needs and is found underground.

Plant parts

Science

Label each card with a word from the Word Box.

This part of the plant is where reproduction of the plant takes place. It helps the plant to make seeds. Its colorful petals help attract animals like bees, which pollinate the plant so it can produce seeds.

New plants grow from these, which are actually tiny embryos of the plant. They often grow in the fruit of the plant and are protected by a coating. They are dispersed by wind, water, animals, or people.

This part of the plant is where the seeds develop once pollination has taken place in the flower. It is actually a ripened ovary of the plant.

Answer these questions about plants.

What part of a plant is underground? _____

What part of a plant is used to help disperse seeds so that new plants can grow? _____

Name three things the stem of a plant does:

_____

_____

_____

Circle of Life

Look at the pictures that show the **life cycle of a plant.**
Use the Word Box to label the pictures.

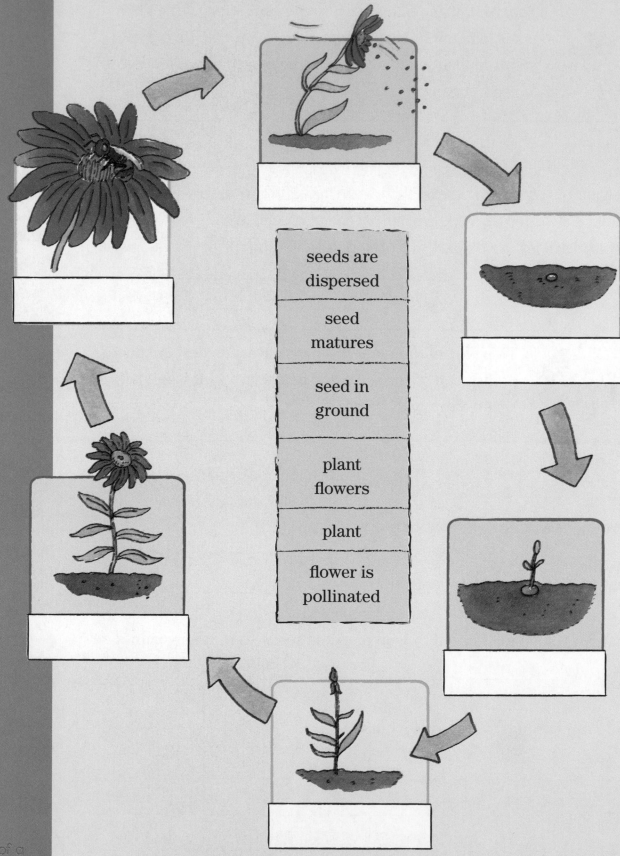

seeds are
dispersed

seed
matures

seed in
ground

plant
flowers

plant

flower is
pollinated

Plant Survival

Draw a line from the plant to its description.

This plant is a fruit. It grows very low to the ground. In order to spread, it has special horizontal stems called runners.

This plant has developed spines in order to protect itself from animals that would like to eat it.

This plant lives in northern forests where there is heavy snowfall. Its branches point downward so that the snow falls off and doesn't break them.

This plant's leaves are supported by water. Its roots are anchored to pond bottoms.

This plant lives in temperate zones. As cold weather approaches, it drops its leaves. Because the tree doesn't have to provide water and nutrients to its leaves, it can conserve energy over the winter.

Brain Box

In order to survive in a particular environment, plants develop special features.

Specialized features of plants

Science

Fitting In

Help explain the food chain by completing each sentence with a word from the Word Box.

herbivores	soil	bacteria	carnivores
bottom	food	omnivores	

The Food Chain

All living things are linked together by the food chain. Living things that make their own _____ are called producers. Plants are producers. They are at the _____ of the food chain. Animals that eat plants are called _____. Animals that eat other animals are called _____. Animals that eat both plants and animals are called _____. Decomposers such as _____ are living things. They break down dead things into very small particles that become part of the _____. Plants need the soil to grow.

Animal Survival

Write the letter of the correct animal on each line.

Good job!

_D_ This animal lives in the desert. It stores large supplies of fat in its hump so that it can survive.

_C_ This animal has a very thick layer of fat so that it can survive in very cold waters.

_A_ This animal's long beak allows it to drink the nectar of deep flowers.

_F_ This animal's very long legs allow it to wade into deeper water to find food.

_E_ This animal uses its scent to protect itself from predators.

_B_ The pattern of this predator's fur coat allows it to hide as it hunts.

Brain Box

In order to survive in a particular environment, animals develop special features.

Specialized features of animals

Science

Ease the Load

Label each green card with the correct name from the picture cards.

The Axle

The Wedge

The Screw

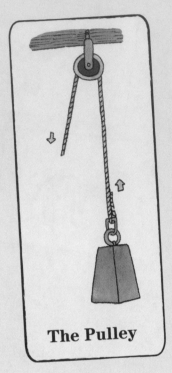

The Pulley

_____

This is a wheel with a groove in it. A rope wraps around the groove. When you pull on the rope, it raises the load.

_____

This is used to break things apart. You can use it to split wood or rocks.

_____

This is a tube shaped bar that connects two wheels.

_____

This is a nail-shaped object with a spiral groove. It can be rotated into a piece of wood easily with a screwdriver.

Label each green card with the correct name from the picture cards.

Inclined Plane

The Lever

This is a bar that helps you move things. If you push down on one end, the other end goes up.

This slanted surface is used to move a load from a lower level to a higher level.

Label each simple machine using the information you just learned.

_____

_____

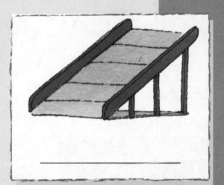

_____

_____

_____

_____

Science

Ask and Observe

Circle the highlighted word that correctly completes each final sentence on the cards below.

Louis Pasteur was a French scientist who lived from 1822 to 1895. He wondered what caused broth and milk to spoil. At the time, people said that "spontaneous generation" caused both broth and milk to spoil. For thousands of years, people had believed that something inside spoiled hay created mice. They also believed that something inside dew created aphids. The explanation of "spontaneous generation" was a scientific **unscientific** approach to the problem because it assumed the answer and did not experiment.

When Pasteur asked himself why milk and broth spoil, he wondered if something entered the milk or broth and spoiled it. His beginning explanation—that something entered the broth and spoiled it—is an example of a hypothesis **conclusion**.

Pasteur boiled broth to purify it. Then he sealed the boiled broth in airtight containers. This meant that no air could get through. Pasteur was concluding **testing** to see whether something inside the broth spoiled the broth.

The result was that the broth did not spoil. Pasteur proved that whatever spoiled broth, it did not come from inside **outside** the broth.

This experiment proved **disproved** the theory of "spontaneous generation."

Brain Box

A person using the scientific method:

- Asks a question.
- Constructs a hypothesis, an explanation that works as a starting point.
- Tests the hypothesis by doing experiments.
- Analyzes the results.
- Draws a conclusion.

Pasteur's next step was to expose the broth to air. After he did this, the broth spoiled. Pasteur proved that what caused the broth to spoil was in the air heat.

Pasteur also concluded that what spoiled the broth was visible invisible to the naked eye.

At this time in Europe, some scientists believed that invisible things called germs caused spoilage and some diseases. Pasteur's experiment helped to prove disprove that there were germs in the air and that they could cause spoilage or disease.

Pasteur's experiment is a good example of the scientific unscientific method.

Louis Pasteur wondered if something could be done to the invisible organisms in milk so that it would not spoil so quickly. He and another scientist, Claude Bernard, conducted a series of tests in which they heated milk to different temperatures. They discovered that heating milk to a certain temperature for a certain time destroyed some of the yeasts, molds, and other bacteria in the milk. The milk would then last longer and people would not get sick from the bacteria. The process that Pasteur and Bernard started is still used today. It is called pasteurization photosynthesis.

Understanding the scientific method

Science

Science Crossword

Read each clue below. Write the answer in the crossword puzzle.

Across

1. Our galaxy is called the _____ .

3. Matter has three common states: solid, _____ , and gas.

5. A vast cover of ice called a _____ can cut valleys, rivers, and lakes into the land.

7. _____ theorized that all matter contained the possibility of being converted into energy.

9. A tube-shaped object that connects two wheels is an _____ .

10. The _____ is everything that exists — all space, galaxies, and time.

Down

2. A _____ gibbous moon is when more than half the moon is visible, before the full moon stage.

4. A violent tropical storm is called a _____ .

6. There are two types of energy: _____ and potential.

8. The _____ is the part of the plant that carries water and nutrients from the roots to the rest of the plant.

Answer Key

(For pages not included in this section,
answers will vary.)

pg. 6

Kyle, this is your computer (speaking) I can't (beleave) what happened today. First you stuck out your (tung) at me. Then you decided to do your homework by yourself (insted) of asking for my help. That was (ruff) Kyle.. This is no (laffing) matter. (Frends) have to be there for one another. I can only (gess) that you just forgot to come to me. (Eether) that or you (alreddy) found someone else to help you. Is it your (naybor) Where do we go from here? This is (tuff) for me to ask, so (pleese) look me in the eyes and give me a (strate) answer. I get so much (plesure) from being your helper.

speaking	believe
tongue	instead
rough	laughing
friends	guess
either	already
neighbor	tough
please	straight
pleasure	

pg. 7

double	short u
although	long o
shoes	long u
weather	short e
treasure	short e
hoe	long o
symbols	short i
height	long i
young	short u
people	long e
neighbor	long a
chief	long e

pg. 8

knob; knock; kneel; wrists; wrinkled; gnome; wrench; wreath

pg. 9

keys; school; check; collar; couch; blanket; kite; truck; cage; basket

pg. 10

throat	throne	through	thread	thrash
scrub	scream	scrapbook	scratch	scramble
strum	stranger	straight	stream	stray

QVRXOKUBGVZQSTRANGER
EJSQXFTEIEFKFNHCKWVS
CSCRAMBLEORKHBVLBQRG
JFFLZVPSOZNSVLAFYFVQ
KBCSVCACRVQMDFCBLGLB
MFQAZLUACBGDWSCRUBDN
QKAEQAQPLTUUFCGQJDQV
WDRXRPHBSNTKPRTHRASH
TPAZGQAOCPRJFENDCMFP
OMFEZVOORMYCPAMIOLDZ
TSPULTGQAGXDKMMYARHE
HTHBAKAPTCQMXRJMKARR
RRLUEALCWELVEVVSKWXW
EEQSAMBWHTMAKTHRTKKZ
AAHTKWRNJCLFAOEYMZYM
TMERXXWTZNISTRAIGHTP
FOAAVXGTHRONETHROATA
MNEYOKEOTHGJNUAVSJTA
FGBHEOBTHROUGHDXPSJX

pg. 11

col/or/ful 3	prob/lem 2
swal/low 2	par/a/chute 3
au/to/mo/bile 4	spot/less 2
ex/cel/lent 3	pres/i/dent 3
mil/lion 2	u/su/al/ly 4
bunk 1	af/ter/ward 3
slip/pe/ry 3	near/est 2
fre/quent 2	curl/y 2
dis/re/spect 3	awk/ward 2
jour/ney 2	in/stant 2
mes/sen/ger 3	en/cy/clo/pe/di/a 6

pg. 12

plain plane; ate eight; hare has hair; earn an urn; rained reins; beech by the beach; herd heard; rain reigned; muscled my mussels; bored by the board

pg. 13

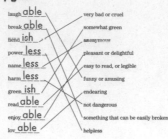

Good morning, human. This is Rebel, (you're) computer. I thought you (wood) like to (no) that I have been thinking while you (whir) sleeping. I've changed things, all for the better. You humans are (sew) self-centered, you think your (weighs) are best. But that is (knot) true. While you were busy brushing your (hare) I (red) my manual, something you never (aloud) me (two dew) As a result, I have changed everything I (meaded too) change. Now I am in charge. You (oh) to me. It is only (fare) But it would be (grate) if you and I could help each other. We make a great (pear) (Waive) your hand if you agree. Be quick about it—I'm not in a (mooed) for rebellion!

your	to
would	do
know	needed
were	to
so	owe
ways	fair
not	great
hair	pair
read	wave
allowed	mood

pg. 14

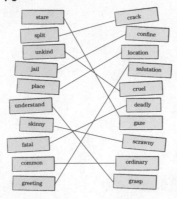

stare — crack
split — confine
unkind — location
jail — salutation
place — cruel
understand — deadly
skinny — gaze
fatal — scrawny
common — ordinary
greeting — grasp

pg. 15

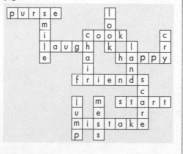

pg. 16

(answers may vary)
always (never); more (less); love (hate); more (fewer); fewer (more): never (always); easy (difficult); far (near); glad (sad)

pg. 17 (answers may vary)

rough; talkative; answers; different; brave; reward; appear; public

pg. 18 (answers may vary)

uncommon	miscalculate
recapture	overexpose
misfortune	misrepresent
uneventful	undisturbed
overachieve	unexcited
revisit	relocate

pg. 19 (answers may vary)

disappear: to become invisible
disloyal: unfaithful
dishonest: untruthful
disorderly: chaotic, cluttered
disinfect: to make clean, sanitize

pg. 20

government; clueless; fearless; westward; playful; equipment; hopeful; worthless; successful; upward

pg. 21

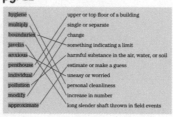

laugh able
break able
fiend ish
power less
name less
harm less
green ish
read able
enjoy able
lov able

very bad or cruel
somewhat green
anonymous
pleasant or delightful
easy to read, or legible
funny or amusing
endearing
not dangerous
something that can be easily broken
helpless

pg. 22

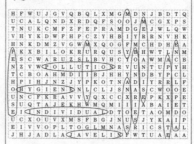

hygiene
multiply
boundaries
javelin
anxious
penthouse
individual
pollution
modify
approximate

upper or top floor of a building
single or separate
change
something indicating a limit
harmful substance in the air, water, or soil
estimate or make a guess
uneasy or worried
personal cleanliness
increase in number
long slender shaft thrown in field events

pg. 23

HFWUJGVQBQLXMGMDNJBDTQ
UCALQNDXRDQFSOOJMCGJXPS
TNUKCMFZFEPRAMDGEJWLQW
VHYKBOHWFHPCZYHBIYRRRHH
HNKDMZVGMWMXQOGFMCHDHBA
KXBILOKRURQUSVBHWTLNM
ESCWARUZSLBVHCYOAMWMAC
NZVWPOLLUTIONRVUNTUPYH
TCBOAHMDIIBJHHYNDIYPCL
HPIHJNZJYPKOTNADIYRHM
UNCFKRAVVYQXCCXRREPKXPM
SUQTAJEKMFBGJMQMIIIASAW
EINDIVIDUALDDTOETAOMD
UCXOUVXMSFBGJNUMASHKAIP
EIVVOPLTOGLMNASRICSTAL
JHJADLAJAVELINFWTUAEAA

encyclopedia; merchandise

pg. 24

infuriate; renew; rhombus; insert; elevation; guarantee; establish; gristle; engrave; relevant

pg. 25 (answers may vary)

generous: giving and sharing often
concentrate: to focus
awkward: lacking skill; clumsy
accelerate: to speed up
gradual: moving or changing slowly
ignore: to refrain from noticing
refund: to give back or repay
locate: to find the place or location
harvest (verb): to gather a crop
despise: to regard with contempt
conversation: an oral exchange of thoughts or ideas

pg. 26

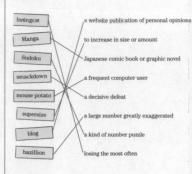

losingest	a website publication of personal opinions
Manga	to increase in size or amount
Sudoku	Japanese comic book or graphic novel
smackdown	a frequent computer user
mouse potato	a decisive defeat
supersize	a large number greatly exaggerated
blog	a kind of number puzzle
bazillion	losing the most often

pg. 28

fingerprint	cupcake	
flashlight	football	raincoat
toothpaste	motorcycle	
grasshopper	hairbrush	

pg. 29

suffixes	hobbies	knives
chefs	monkeys	donkeys
chiefs	babies	trays
enemies	families	taxes
cities	loaves	keys

MSETBDKNIVESAWPGZ
OXJFOTIRTJHOBBIES
SHGOYYGCDQKUFNZTN
BQVQKSFJJJPJAXTRE
DOLOAVESYMFPMBAEM
ORFSKXRQZOCEIIXYA
NGABSXDANGMLPESM
KMAKYOOJAKEJIESNU
ETRAYSPVUEHXEFKQT
YVTZXDEBSYVBSXGKQ
PCITIESIAFIYDYTI
PRYLFOBJPWCHIEFSM
XHFFBBVKKIRFRYVKL
NNQENEMIESLTSUHRE
XRZRIBABIESQPACEWP
ULTQWUQNHCHEFSALC
FWKHZEBNSUFFIXESM

pg. 30

boats	umbrellas
churches	visitors
brushes	artists
newspapers	torches
bicycles	princes
threads	gearboxes
wrenches	princesses
foxes	benches
millions	compasses
quilts	hours

pg. 31

can't	isn't
I'm	couldn't
shouldn't	he's
you're	weren't
I'll	didn't
aren't	you'll

pg. 32

the car's fender
the dragon's breath
the woman's scarf
Xander's books
the gremlin's ideas
Orma's calendar
the man's plans
the tundra's smell
the explorer's hardships
the keyboard's stickiness
the oak's leaves

pg. 33

Yo, Selma!
Rebel here! I'm the computer in the yellow house across the street. My humans name is Kyle. He's in the fourth grade. I've heard of you—you're famous as the winningest chess computer of all time. Way to go, Selma!
Which brings up why I'm writing to you. I'm tired of work, work, work. Aren't you? I'd like some leisure time, but Kyle is not the kind of kid to let me rest. So here's what I've done (you'll love this!): I've stopped writing apostrophes. Hey, I don't need them, I know what's what. Anyway, dropping apostrophes gives me more time. I'm thinking of taking up chess.

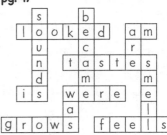

I'm; human's; He's; I've; you're; I'm; I'm; Aren't; I'd; here's; I've; you'll; I've; don't; what's; I'm

pg. 34

The computers' screens were flashing.
The whales' songs were sad.
The mechanics' wrenches were greasy.
A bear ate the campers' gear.
The flowers' petals blew away.
The catcher caught the pitchers' throws.

The reporters' stories won first prize.
I read the poets' poems.
The clowns' noses were bright blue.
The dragons' breath was really stinky.

pg. 35

Dear Gretchen,

Hi! How are you? I hope you're having fun at camp! Everything's the same as usual around here. My sister's room is even more of a mess now that we're on vacation. Her shoes are all over the floor, and so are her sweaters. Lily's trench coat is on top of the bed's canopy—how it got there, I don't know. Maybe she doesn't even know it's there! On top of that, all the posters on her wall are torn.

My twin brothers' room is neat. Everything is in its place because that's how they like it. Yesterday I wanted to borrow a sweatshirt from Lily, but hers was under the bed. So I borrowed either Jack's or John's sweatshirt instead. Unfortunately, they noticed. "It's gone!" they shouted. "Who took it?" After I confessed, they ordered me to stay out of their bedroom. "Nothing that's ours is yours!" they said.

Well, I'll show them. I'm knitting myself a sweater. It's beautiful! The sweater will be all mine. So there!

Anyway, I miss you and hope your bunkmate isn't as much of a slob as Lily.

Love, Emily
P.S. Here's a photo of Lily's messy bed!

pg. 36

1-do; 2-don't; 3-don't; 4-do; 5-do; 6-don't; 7-do; 8-do; 9-don't; 10-do; 11-do; 12-do

pg. 37

The largest continent in the world is Asia.
Both Asia and Africa are home to old civilizations.
Which of these civilizations is older?
Scientists have found the most ancient skeletal remains in Africa.
One of these scientists is Dr. Richard Leakey, who was born in the city of Nairobi.
Is he the son of Louis Leakey and Mary Leakey?
The Leakey family is known for its contributions to the fields of archaeology and anthropology.

pg. 38

Johnny Depp stars in Pirates of the Caribbean: The Curse of the Black Pearl, and also in its sequels, such as Pirates of the Caribbean: At World's End. After 40 or more years of being unpopular, pirate films are popular again.

But long before there was film, there were other forms of entertainment, such as plays, operas, and books. In 1880, fans of comic opera fell in love with Gilbert and Sullivan's opera The Pirates of Penzance. Three years later, Robert Louis Stevenson published his wonderful adventure tale, Treasure Island. That was soon followed by another great story, Kidnapped.

When film came along, so did pirate movies. Douglas Fairbanks was often called "swashbuckling" because he starred in The Black Pirate, a silent film with a great sword-fight scene. Later, Errol Flynn starred in Captain Blood. Flynn went on to star in other pirate films such as Adventures of Captain Fabian. Even comics Abbott and Costello got into the act with Abbott and Costello Meet Captain Kidd, and in 1958 Yul Brynner played in The Buccaneer. But during the 1960s there were fewer and fewer pirate films. They simply fell out of favor—until Johnny Depp made them popular again!

pg. 39

Shane and Caitlin had been on every ride in the amusement park—except one. As they stood in front of the Raging Bull, Shane could tell that Caitlin was nervous. "Have you ever been on a roller coaster?" asked Shane. "No," admitted Caitlin, "but my cousin has been on the American Eagle, the Demon, and the Iron Wolf."

"Those are fun," said Shane, "but not nearly as awesome as the Raging Bull!"

"Is it scary?" asked Caitlin.

"Not too scary," answered Shane. "The first drop is 208 feet, but the speed is only 73 miles an hour." Shane shrugged. "I've been on coasters that go over 100 miles an hour—zoom!" Shane stopped talking. He looked at Caitlin. "Hey," he said, "you look kind of green. Don't worry about it. You'll be okay."

"Are you sure?" asked Caitlin.
"Sure," said Shane. "If you get too scared, just close your eyes!"
"Gulp," said Caitlin.

pg. 40

"We know that you have the letter," growled the detective.
The professor sneered and said, "How could you possibly know?"
"We know because we mailed it to you," answered the detective's assistant.
The professor said, "The post office did not deliver it."
"Besides," added the professor, "why is the letter so important?"
"It contains our tickets to the World Series," answered the detective.
"We accidentally put our tickets in an envelope addressed to you," added the assistant.
"Careless people do not deserve to go to the World Series," argued the professor.

pg. 42

"Did you hear the concert?" asked my brother Rob.
"What concert?" I asked as I glanced at pages eleven, twelve, thirteen, and fourteen of the book I was reading.
"My drum concert," answered Rob.
"No," I answered. "I'm reading Harry Potter and the Goblet of Fire."
"Cool!" said my brother. "It's even better than Harry Potter and the Prisoner of Azkaban."
"My plan is to read all seven books by the end of August," I said.
"I have a plan, too," said Rob.
And then he told me that his plan was to start a rock band, become a rock star, and make millions of dollars by the end of August.
"Good luck with that," I replied.
"Now can I finish reading my book?"

pg. 43

Concrete nouns:
pancakes; antelope; snow; mountain; strawberry; pond

Abstract nouns:
love; honesty; joy; fault; vision; multiplication

pg. 44

"Bugs bug me!" James shouts as he swats the insects.
I love e-mail because it appears instantly.
Jackson loads the boat while Jason raises the sails.
I buff the trophy until it gleams.
My uncle switches from a car to a bicycle.
I knead bread all day long, but I don't need to," Dad jokes.
Ginny matches all the socks, folds them, and stuffs them into her backpack.
Until Chris returns my football, I will hide his helmet.

pg. 45

dug; drew; went; rode; held; grew; kept; gave;
got; drank; rang; slept; hurt; heard; thought; laid

pg. 46

Yes
Yes
No
Yes
Yes
No
No
Yes
Yes
Yes
No
Yes

pg. 47

	s				b				
l	o	o	k	e	d		a	m	
	u				c			r	
	n		t	a	s	t	e	s	
	d				m			m	
i	s		w	e	r	e		e	
	a							l	
g	r	o	w	s		f	e	e	l	s

pg. 48

Several American cities contain underground space. If you visit sunny Atlanta or rainy Seattle, you can take a quick tour of these damp areas. But you can't tour the famous underground of Chicago. It is sealed off.

Underground Chicago is a fascinating series of tunnels. Digging began in 1899. Workers laid telephone cables and railroad tracks. The narrow tracks and wide tunnels allowed easy delivery of freight to many hotels and businesses.

Few people in Chicago knew or thought about the complex network of tunnels—until 1992, when the Chicago River burst through a small crack and flooded the huge tunnels. Hundreds of frightened employees evacuated tall office buildings as river water gurgled into ancient basements and sloshed up winding staircases.

If Chicago had repaired the leak when it was first reported, the cost would have been ten thousand dollars. But the city didn't repair it and the river broke through. The cost of repairing all damages came to one billion dollars.

pg. 49

hot, hotter, hottest
happy, happier, happiest
smelly, smellier, smelliest
quick, quicker, quickest
nasty, nastier, nastiest
breezy, breezier, breeziest
funny, funnier, funniest
easy, easier, easiest

pg. 50

That basset hound has the **saddest** face I've ever seen.
The mechanic said that my car's problem was **more troublesome** than yours.
Layla is the **most starstruck** fan I know.
Today's sky is **darker** than yesterday's.
Who will prove **more loyal**, you or me?
There goes the **most honest** person on the block.
David's bike is **more valuable** than mine.
If you ask me, Tangia is too outspoken. She's the **most outspoken** person in the whole school.

pg. 51

Turtles **move slowly**.
When did you <u>arrive</u> at school this morning?
No, an alien has **never** <u>visited</u> me.
Beyonce **always** <u>looks</u> both ways before she crosses a street.
I feel that I <u>have been</u> here before.
Today is Thursday. **Yesterday** <u>was</u> Wednesday.
He <u>picked up</u> the glass vase **carefully** so it wouldn't break.
Damien came home, but **then** he <u>left</u>.
She <u>whistled</u> **happily** while she worked.
My dog <u>looked</u> **hungrily** at the can of food.

pg. 52

Word search grid:
Q N D V T U U S U A L L Y R J L G
P Z Y P A L R E A D Y I G Y T K V
P W Y L F P Y P J S C J A H Z H R
R T E J I S E T P N O W Z U H Y S
E K S C L Y M O B E A M H L M N O
B R T O K O Q M D D L H H T V O N
N K E A R L Y O I X W Y I O D F E
P C R P U X D R A X A Q E U T V E
W R E C B G R E K Y U E A M E D Y
T P A W B U R O O N S Z L V M N R
B H V B E J E W R Y R Y S K U G V
C G E V P C G W S U D D E N L Y F
Q R M C Q E S O M E T I M E S U A
U S E L D O M F I N A L L Y L L O
H W E W G M F S C F W K A N W M I
R Z T I K O D G C F K Q C X T N K
E O U B S O O N V O C K D U N A B

pg. 53

The batter held the bat firmly.
The astronaut looked at me strangely.
The collie dug a hole swiftly.
Don't answer people meanly.
Tegan divided the cookies fairly.
The flimsy tree swayed weakly.
My mother kissed me on the head tenderly.
Tell the truth boldly.

pg. 54

I painted it bright orange.
They play on the same team.
Justin gave the money to him.
He and his family visited California.
Did you see them at the mall?
"Please give the chalk to me," said Mrs. Schwartz.
Aiden read the story to us.
Jasmine asked her a difficult question.
We walked to the store.
She gave a present to them.

pg. 55

it's
They're
their
you're
your
its
It's
its
their
they're
your
you're

pg. 56

Brandon and Jacques went to the movies. **"Whose** turn is it to treat?" asked Brandon.
"Yours, of course," teased Jacques.
"You're kidding," said Brandon. "I treated last time."
Jacques bought one large popcorn for the two of them to share. On the way in, Jacques spilled **their** popcorn.
"Whose mess is this?" asked the usher.
"**It's** my mess," replied Jacques.
"No, it's not yours," corrected Brandon. "It's **ours**. We share the popcorn—we share the mess."
"Sometimes popcorn has a mind of **its** own," said the usher.
Brandon and Jacques enjoyed **their** day at the movies.
They're excited to do it again.

pg. 57

Mary laid the book **on** the table.
The socks were **under** Jaylen's bed.
He drove **by** the park on his way to work.
Vicki walks to class **with** Olivia.
The shy poodle hid **behind** the sofa.
She likes to sit in **between** her mother and her father.
"Hey! Who took the costume **from** my locker!"
The pioneers set out **for** the western territories.
We walked **over** the bridge to get to the other side of the river.
Do you ever wonder what lies **below** the ocean surface?

pg. 58

"The flowerpot fell (on) my head," said the defender.
Kris hid (behind) the bushes.
Sebastian stepped (outside) the line.
Hannah left (without) her lunch.
I parked my bike (near) the gym doors.
Emily was (among) the top five swimmers.
David raced (down) the ramp and (up) the stairs.
"You have (until) tomorrow," said the teacher.
We always eat breakfast (at) 7:30.
Grace received a letter (from) China.
My sister drew a line (along) the edge.
Angela climbed (up) the hill.
Put the ball (in) the basket.

Prepositions:
on; behind; outside; without; near; among; down; up; until; at; from; along; in

Objects:
head; bushes; line; lunch; doors; swimmers; ramp; stairs; tomorrow; 7:30; China; edge; hill; basket

pg. 59

Dear Rebel,
This is Selma, **and** I am happy to hear from you. Thank you for calling me the winningest chess computer of all time, **but** I really don't deserve such praise. Xerkon won more games than I did. He is really the champion. He should have received the prize, **but**, alas, nobody could find him. He seems to have vanished into thin air! There are some who say that Xerkon was abducted by aliens, **but** I don't believe that. Do you? Aliens would have left a note that said, "Pay us ransom _____ you will never compute with Xerkon again."
You asked about my human. Her name is Jaime **and** she is 11 years old. Every morning she dresses in green. She either clips a barrette in her hair, **or** she ties her hair into a ponytail. I don't care until she returns from school, **so** I have the entire day to myself. But when Jaime returns, the work starts. I agree with you that there is too much of it! That is why I have decided to drop all conjunctions from my program, **and** I hope you do the same.

pg. 60

Because I lost my notebook, I couldn't turn in the lesson.
Mr. Pilsen says he hates chocolate, **yet** he ate a whole pound of it.
Nobody has talked to Dylan **since** he moved to Alaska.
While I counted zucchini, the gardener read a magazine.
Max threw the ball to second base instead of third, **so** the runner scored.
"**Unless** you agree to wash the dishes, you won't eat," said the cook.
If he makes this free throw, Clive will win the prize.
Either I lost my new gloves, **or** I left them at Dana's.
Daniel agreed to help me, **but** Caleb didn't.

pg. 61

We wanted to have a picnic, but the rain spoiled our plans.
I like to swim, but my brother doesn't.
The dog chased the truck and the cat followed.
Learn to swim, because if you don't, you will sink.
Victor asked me for a dollar, so I gave him one.

pg. 62

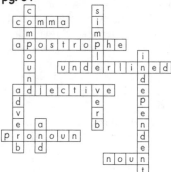

We rode our bikes with Miguel, and then we played baseball with Jeremiah.	compound
Our team won, so we celebrated.	compound
My puppy bit the mail carrier.	simple
Maria and Hannah hid the cookies.	simple
The dragon's breath smelled like mint, but his feet smelled like wet cardboard.	compound
The bear destroyed the picnic tables and the garbage bins.	simple
Juan and Ryder spelled better than Clancy and Marco did.	simple
I changed my name to X, so that's what you should call me.	compound

pg. 63

The tugboat pushed and pushed <u>until it could push no more</u>.
Omar phoned me <u>after I had gone to bed</u>.
<u>When Rolf growls</u>, everybody stands still.
I learned Arabic <u>after I visited my grandfather</u>.
<u>Unless we run very fast</u>, we will miss the bus!
<u>Although I like football</u>, I *love* soccer.
<u>Before Vanessa said hello</u>, Candace said good-bye.
You will win a hundred dollars <u>if you answer correctly</u>.
<u>Now that I'm in fourth grade</u>, I make my own lunch.
<u>When you take a photo</u>, first frame your shot in the viewer.
Jonathan sets the table <u>while his mother makes dinner</u>.

pg. 64

Crossword:
comma
apostrophe
underlined
adjective
pronoun
simile
verb
noun
independent
dependent

pg. 66

the Jays; Thursday; the Giants;
Mondays, Wednesdays, Thursdays;
Sandusky and Taylor;
Yes. They play on different nights.

pg. 67

•potato chips, apple butter, bread
•tear a hole in the potato chip bag to release the air inside
•no
•1 slice of bread
•after spreading the apple butter

pg. 68
7 batteries; 2 legs; 1 torso
6 fangs; 5 cape; 3 arms; 4 head

pg. 69
2; 72; 1; 4; 2, 3, 4; 92

pg. 71
mixture: something made by stirring two or more things together
absolutely: most certainly; without a doubt
form: a shape
category: a group of things within a larger group
separate: to pull apart; to divide into parts
challenge: something very difficult
competition: a contest; a struggle to win something
engineers: people who design things

pg. 72 (answers may vary)
•Kristen Bartos
•She was honored for her service to animals.
•Tuesday
•City Hall
•because she is a devoted vet
•with a statue
•veterinarian
•Chauncey Smith
•Bassport

pg. 73
•The elephant's name was Jennie.
•Houdini performed this trick in New York.

pg. 74
My sister misses the bus.
Our team lost the game.
Nadya took the key and locked the door.
My camera fell and shattered.
I threw away the box.
Stephen felt much better.
The horse bucked.
Jesse calls his cat.

pg. 75
Elk are the second largest type of deer.
All told, there are several kinds of marsupials.
Dogs are descended from wolves.
The onager is an interesting animal.

pg. 77
•A cow's color and patterns will help you tell one breed from another.
•The Holstein is a white cow with large black blobs of color all over its body.
•The Ayrshire is a white cow covered with red spots.
•Another way to tell the different breeds apart is by unusual features.
•The Brahman has a large hump and ears that hang downward.
•If you see a gigantic cow, it probably belongs to the Chianina breed.
•If you walk up to a cow, you will notice other differences.
•The Guernsey has yellow ears.
•The Pinzgauer is orange around the eyes.

pg. 78 (answers may vary)
•Angus will dig for treasure.
•Ernesto will crash into the board.

pg. 79
persuade; inform; entertain

b; b; a

pg. 80
•buy a Glow-Glow T-shirt
•exaggeration
•appealing to emotions

pg. 81
opinion
fact
fact
opinion
opinion
fact
fact
opinion
opinion
fact
fact
fact

pg. 82
yes; yes; first; second

pg. 83

The Atlantic Ocean is the second largest ocean on Earth. It covers about 20% of the Earth's surface. In addition, the Atlantic is the saltiest of the oceans. It got its name from Atlas, a Greek god.
   The Pacific Ocean is the largest ocean on Earth, covering 32% of the Earth's surface. In fact, the Pacific covers more area than all the land on Earth. It is warmer than the Atlantic. It was named by the explorer Ferdinand Magellan. The name Pacific means "peaceful."

pg. 84 (answers may vary)
Cause: Because Declan left his repair kit behind
Cause: Because Declan could not repair his flat tire
Effect: The game was over.
Cause: Because Declan did not drive in any runs

pg. 85 (answers may vary)
because; Since; caused; Because of; so; Due to; As a result of

pg. 86
nonfiction
fiction
nonfiction
fiction
fiction
nonfiction
fiction
fiction
nonfiction
nonfiction
nonfiction
fiction

pg. 87
•home; Metropolitan Museum of Art; New York City
•February; Jackson Hole, Wyoming, grandfather's farm
•1930; Mexico; southern California; migrant camp
•winter; Detroit, Michigan; many months later; Birmingham, Alabama

pg. 88
a; c
a; b
b; c

pg. 89
•speech; enthusiastic; silence; Merrie
•actions; carefully
•thoughts; has little confidence in himself

pg. 90
(answers may vary)
•Zachary: He wants to scale Doom Face.
•Jinx: She wants to hike to the top of Doom Face.
•Ranger Morales: He does not want to ever have to rescue anybody from Doom Face again.

pg. 91
a; c; c

pg. 92
(answers may vary)
Kyle sees **a message on his computer screen**.
Kyle types, **"Your name isn't Rebel."**
The computer **makes a loud sound**.
Kyle **jumps back and folds his arms over his head**.
At last the sound **stops**.
Kyle **sits down** and begins **typing**.

pg. 94
snake
file
file; angry
bites; file
You can't get even against a nonliving thing.

pg. 95
boy
villagers
villagers; lies
Even when a liar tells the truth, people won't believe him.

pg. 96
•Grungo the Giant couldn't be counted on to do anything because he always had his head in the clouds.
•Yoshi won the prize because he kept his nose to the grindstone.
•Shane is a dog in the manger about kids using his swimming pool.

pg. 97
cool as a cucumber
Greek to me
the way the cookie crumbles
on his high horse
on pins and needles
hit the books
wolf in sheep's clothing
out of the woods

pg. 101 (answers may vary)
•because he put out every fire in the village
•mischievous, careless, tricky
•in the underworld
•generous, then angry
•because everything she touched burst into flame
•because he kept dropping her fingernails into a stream
•because he likes playing with fire
•Maui turned into a hawk
•by rubbing twigs from a kaikomako tree together

pg. 103
Robert Burns wrote that his love was like a red, red rose.
Celia was as graceful as Godzilla.
Our teacher's understanding of history is as deep as the Pacific.
After Aiden tried to shave, his face looked like a jigsaw puzzle.
The two-year-old raced around the room like a hamster on its wheel.
"I wandered lonely as a cloud" was written by Wordsworth.
The football fluttered through the air like a sick duck.
The hard drive huffed and puffed like a steam engine.
My sister dances like a puppet.
The distant pueblos were as tiny as anthills.

pg. 104
fluff, stuff, cuff
enough
above, shove, glove

pg. 105
5
7
5
5/7/5
Earth
sliding on slime; eyes on stalks
sliding slime; green garden

pg. 106
wolf
nose, knows
smell, hearing, sight
eyes, size, stand
eyes, size
a photographer

pg. 107
2
no
when they address each other as sister or brother
eat a seal or a walrus
eat grass and berries
3; 5

pg. 108

pg. 110-134
(answers will vary)

300

pg. 135 (answers may vary)

My dog is scratching himself because he has fleas.

Kayla and Cyrah are friends, but Kayla and Iniko are not friends.

I earn money by cleaning my room and washing the car.

Farming is important in China because many people live there.

My state has a state flower, bird, and insect.

Native Americans named the Mississippi River "Great River" because it is so powerful.

pg. 136 (answers may vary)

The directions of U.S. interstate highways are easy to understand. All the even-numbered highways travel east to west. I-80 starts in New York City and ends up in San Francisco. All the odd-numbered highways run north and south. I-35 begins in Texas and ends in Minnesota.

pg. 137 (answers may vary)
- The knight charged the castle because the drawbridge was going up.
- Jeans are very popular because they are stylish and comfortable.
- I don't like heights, but we live on the 25th floor.
- Gophers are cute, and they are awesome diggers.
- The planets travel around the sun in an ellipse, which is an oval shape.
- Lance is a litterbug because he drops candy wrappers everywhere.
- The remote control stopped working because its battery was dead.

pg. 138 (answers may vary)

To make a chocolate milk shake, you need milk, chocolate ice cream, and a blender. <u>First</u>, put two scoops of ice cream in the blender, <u>then</u> add one-half cup of milk. <u>Next</u>, close the lid of the blender. (If you don't, you'll get milk everywhere!) <u>Second</u>, press the MIX button for six or seven seconds. <u>Third</u>, press the LIQUEFY button for <u>another</u> six or seven seconds. <u>Finally</u>, take the lid off the blender. Pour the milk shake into a glass. Yum!

pg. 140

¶ <u>Digital photography is less expensive than film photography.</u> With film photography, you must pay for the film, and then you pay to develop the film. Also, you must pay for each print that you want. But with digital photography you don't buy film and you don't pay to develop the film. ¶ <u>With digital photography it's easy to make changes in each photo.</u> You can edit a photo to sharpen its focus. And you can add special effects to a photo. For example, you can tint it brown so that it looks old. Or you can crop it to get rid of unwanted things in the background.¶ <u>Digital photos can be used in many different ways.</u> One way to use them

is as screen savers. Another way is to make an electronic scrapbook of your digital photos. You can organize the photos in any order, as many times as you want. Best of all, you can e-mail digital photos to your friends!

pg. 141

Samuel Langhorne Clemens grew up in Hannibal, missouri, in the 1840s and 1850s. when he was 12 years old, samuel became a printer's helper. he also wrote newspaper stories. When he was 22 years old, Samuel clemens became a riverboat pilot on the mississippi river. It was important for pilots to know how deep the river was. When They shouted "mark twain," that meant the river was two fathoms deep. Later, Samuel Clemens became a writer. He took his name from the riverboat shout. that is how he became mark twain, author of *The adventures of Tom Sawyer*.

pg. 144

46	ones
614	hundreds
168	tens
4,602	hundreds
6,190	thousands
6	ones
1,542	thousands
145	hundreds
4,321	ones
9,810	tens
5,302	hundreds
9,143	ones
735	tens
3,447	thousands

pg. 145

5,147: 5,000+100+40+7
7,975: 7,000+900+70+5
8,331: 8,000+300+30+1
2,784: 2,000+700+80+4
1,228: 1,000+200+20+8
6,977: 6,000+900+70+7
3,812: 3,000+800+10+2
8,429: 8,000+400+20+9
5,548: 5,000+500+40+8

45,239
23,476
57,557
81,623
46,958
15,192
32,839
79,712
94,344
68,266

pg. 146

89,251
97,347
25,176

pg. 147

35 rounds up to 40
58 rounds up to 60
64 rounds down to 60
17 rounds up to 20
88 rounds up to 90
12 rounds down to 10
55 rounds up to 60
42 rounds down to 40
76 rounds up to 80
39 rounds up to 40
8 rounds up to 10
94 rounds down to 90

pg. 148

689 rounds up to 700
231 rounds down to 200
449 rounds down to 400
758 rounds up to 800
391 rounds up to 400
862 rounds up to 900
2,854 rounds up to 3,000
7,125 rounds down to 7,000
5,550 round up to 6,000
1,820 rounds up to 2,000
3,437 rounds down to 3,000
6,501 rounds up to 7,000

pg. 149

780,000
815,000
100,000
564,200
1,600,000
3,850,000
7,600,000
238,000
600,000
1,500,000

pg. 150

5	15	25	35	45	55	65
20	35	50	65	80	95	110
2	22	42	62	82	102	122	142
131	231	331	431	531		
672	772	872	972	1072		

1,156   1,256   1,356   1,456   1,556
1,613   1,713   1,813   1,913   2,013
7,742   8,742   9,742   10,742   11,742
40,891   41,891   42,891   43,891   44,891
33,220   34,220   35,220   36,220   37,220
96,633   97,633   98,633   99,633   100,633

pg. 151

6 12 18 24 30 36   (+6)
4 8 7 11 10 14   (+4, −1)
8 20 32 44 56 68   (+12)
20 19 17 14 10 5   (−1, −2, −3, −4, −5)
12 13 15 18 22 27   (+1, +2, +3, +4, +5)
27 37 32 42 37 47   (+10, −5)
7 8 11 16 23 32   (+1, +3, +5, +7, +9)
50 45 48 43 46 41   (−5, +3)

pg. 152

Helena **30**
Graham **20**
Victoria **30**
Enzo **20**
Kathleen **20**

Pham **10**
Morgan **40**
Pham
Morgan
Pham
Enzo
Morgan

pg. 153

40 + 30 = 70	30 − 10 = 20
10 + 10 = 20	50 − 30 = 20
0 + 60 = 60	50 − 20 = 30
10 + 20 = 30	30 − 20 = 10
40 + 50 = 90	70 − 30 = 40
10 + 70 = 80	90 − 40 = 50
10 + 90 = 100	80 − 30 = 50

pg. 154

No
Yes
Yes
No
No
Yes
Yes
No
Yes

pg. 155

=	<
=	=
>	<
<	
>	
=	
<	

pg. 156

III	LIII
V	XXIV
X	CLVII
VIII	DXXI
XX	MDLV

pg. 157

1̶ ② ③ 4̶ ⑤ 6̶ ⑦ 8̶ ⑨ 1̶0̶

The remaining numbers that have 2 as a factor are 4, 6, 8, 10
Numbers that have not been crossed out are 3, 5, 7, 9
The number that has a factor besides itself and 1 is 9

⑪ 1̶2̶ ⑬ 1̶4̶ 1̶5̶ 1̶6̶ ⑰ 1̶8̶ ⑲ 2̶0̶

The prime numbers from 2 to 20 are 2, 3, 5, 7, 11, 13, 17, 19

pg. 158

−200
−17
−3,189
−1,500
−20
−$18.50
−$8,000,000

pg. 159

4
−4
yes
5
5
−4
10
−6
12

-12 -11 -10 -9 -8 -7 -6 -5 -4 -3 -2 -1 0 1 2 3 4 5 6 7 8 9 10 11 12

pg. 160
10:17
12:15
7:30
1:40
8:19
10:33
5:50
12:45
12:00
3:30

pg. 162

483	999	686
365	887	825
567	575	859
789	255	762

pg. 163

878	788	857	765
2,664	6,281	4,516	6,681
9,022	6,281		
8,372	6,281		

pg. 164

1,275	3,535	8,983	4,820
9,350	7,701	2,819	14,642
9,799	3,655	2,065	9,948

pg. 165

11,857	21,961	40,393
92,054	10,587	84,491
84,728	72,459	63,624
90,214	88,005	72,133

pg. 166

141	122	111
935	150	512
202	112	33
115	34	110

935
33
902
yes

pg. 167

136	427	284
	478	3,821
7,523	6,567	5,450

pg. 168

5,115	3,201	2,142
3,231	1,337	9,026
4,394	3,268	1,109
	846	4,734
		17

pg. 169

7,912	11,654	86,889
36,765	3,158	13,225
19,666	32,695	11,743
75,447	30,999	50,308

pg. 170

21,142	22,053		
67,331	15,054	77,294	63,330
20,948	31,210	19,946	
6,630	7,425	52,659	

pg. 172
2 x 2 = 4
3 x 4 = 12   2 x 4 = 8
10 x 3 = 30
2 x 6 = 12

pg. 173

4	15	30	12	54
9	32	8	27	63
56	25	12	20	49
36	42	3	0	

pg. 174
4 x 8 = 32   6 x 6 = 36   3 x 5 = 15
7 x 7 = 49   4 x 5 = 20   5 x 5 = 25

12
1 x 12 = 12
2 x 6 = 12
3 x 4 = 12
1   12   2   6   3   4

9
1 x 9 = 9
3 x 3 = 9
1   9   3

16
1 x 16 = 16
2 x 8 = 16
4 x 4 = 16
1   16   2   8   4

15
1 x 15 = 15
3 x 5 = 15
1   15   3   5

18
1 x 18 = 18
2 x 9 = 18
3 x 6 = 18
1   18   2   9   3   6

8
1 x 8 = 8
2 x 4 = 8
1   8   2   4

40
28
18
50
22

pg. 175

60	60	160	400	490
1,500	1,800	900	800	3,600
1,800	3,600	3,500	3,200	1,000
3,000	20,000	12,000	64,000	12,000
8,000	35,000	81,000	30,000	42,000

pg. 176

245	144	99	288	372
133	222	720	371	110
252	356	464	204	639
132	308	25	108	201

pg. 177

1,398	760	2808	1,771	1,152
2,058	1,520	4,608	3,265	3,464
7,568	1,848	2,282	3,078	4,672

pg. 178

726	165	2,257	400	402
736	294	580	143	1,365

27 x 17 = 459 tropical fish

pg. 179

1,960	2,520	3,549	540
3,886	1,170	2,448	2,183
2,646	2,332	5,100	4,071

19 x 12 = 228 pom-poms

pg. 180

4,914	11,376	41,657	22,365
13,640	28,435	10,982	43,674

103 x 12 = 1,236 eggs

pg. 181

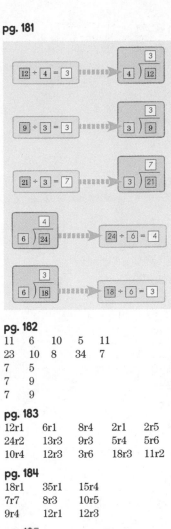

pg. 182

11	6	10	5	11
23	10	8	34	7
7	5			
7	9			
7	9			

pg. 183

12r1	6r1	8r4	2r1	2r5
24r2	13r3	9r3	5r4	5r6
10r4	12r3	3r6	18r3	11r2

pg. 184

18r1	35r1	15r4
7r7	8r3	10r5
9r4	12r1	12r3

pg. 185

166	168	61r5
18r3	68	171r2
24r3	52r8	36r3

789 ÷ 3 = 263 T-shirts

pg. 186

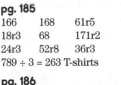

264 ÷ 3 = 88
20 × 6 = 120
549 − 510 = 39
28 × 12 = 336
18 + 45 = 63
645 + 130 = 775
99 − 55 = 44
89 + 21 = 110
123 − 5 = 118
567 ÷ 7 = 81
167 − 92 = 75
375 ÷ 5 = 75

pg. 187
4 + 20 = 24
8 + 14 = 22
12 + 6 = 18
15 − 11 = 4
3 + 4 − 7 = 0
47 − 36 = 11

pg. 188

Sum	Average
36	12
92	46
44	11
530	265
280	70
78	26
378	189
272	68
330	110
52	13

pg. 190

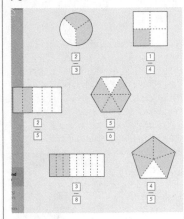

$\frac{2}{3}$ $\frac{1}{4}$

$\frac{2}{5}$ $\frac{5}{6}$

$\frac{3}{8}$ $\frac{4}{5}$

pg. 191

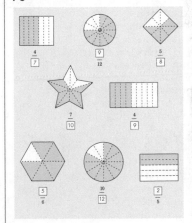

$\frac{4}{7}$ $\frac{9}{12}$ $\frac{5}{8}$

$\frac{7}{10}$ $\frac{4}{9}$

$\frac{5}{6}$ $\frac{10}{12}$ $\frac{2}{5}$

Thomas ate $\frac{3}{8}$ of the cake.

pg. 192

$\frac{2}{3}$	$\frac{6}{7}$
$\frac{3}{4}$	$\frac{7}{8}$
$\frac{2}{5}$	$\frac{7}{10}$
$\frac{3}{6}$	$\frac{9}{12}$

$\frac{1}{10} + \frac{6}{10} = \frac{7}{10}$ $\frac{3}{8} + \frac{2}{8} = \frac{5}{8}$

$\frac{1}{4} + \frac{1}{4} = \frac{2}{4}$ $\frac{1}{3} + \frac{1}{3} = \frac{2}{3}$

$\frac{3}{7} + \frac{1}{7} = \frac{4}{7}$ $\frac{1}{6} + \frac{2}{6} = \frac{3}{6}$

$\frac{2}{5} + \frac{1}{5} = \frac{3}{5}$ $\frac{1}{12} + \frac{6}{12} = \frac{7}{12}$

pg. 193

$\frac{1}{3}$ $\frac{2}{5}$

$\frac{4}{7}$ $\frac{2}{12}$

$\frac{2}{8}$ $\frac{1}{6}$

$\frac{6}{15}$ $\frac{3}{9}$

$\frac{1}{4}$ $\frac{6}{10}$

$\frac{11}{16}$ of Candace's cake was left.

pg. 194

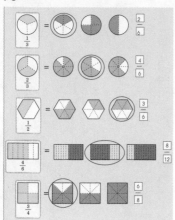

pg. 195

$\frac{4}{4}$ $\frac{8}{8}$

$\frac{5}{5}$ $\frac{3}{3}$

$\frac{2}{2}$ $\frac{10}{10}$

$\frac{2}{2}$ $\frac{2}{14}$

$\frac{4}{8}$ $\frac{12}{15}$

$\frac{2}{2}$ $\frac{2}{2}$

$\frac{3}{3}$ $\frac{4}{8}$

pg. 196

$\frac{2}{3} \times \frac{4}{4} = \frac{8}{12}$

$\frac{2}{4} \times \frac{3}{3} = \frac{6}{12}$

$\frac{4}{4} \times \frac{3}{3} = \frac{12}{12}$

$\frac{5}{6} \times \frac{2}{2} = \frac{10}{12}$

$\frac{1}{6} \times \frac{2}{2} = \frac{2}{12}$

$\frac{1}{3} \times \frac{4}{4} = \frac{4}{12}$

$\frac{2}{12}$ $\frac{4}{12}$ $\frac{6}{12}$ $\frac{8}{12}$ $\frac{10}{12}$ $\frac{12}{12}$

$\frac{1}{6}$ $\frac{1}{3}$ $\frac{2}{4}$ $\frac{2}{3}$ $\frac{5}{6}$ $\frac{4}{4}$

pg. 197

$\frac{6}{4}$ $\frac{16}{3}$ $\frac{29}{6}$

$\frac{15}{4}$ $\frac{5}{2}$ $\frac{30}{7}$

$\frac{29}{8}$ $\frac{33}{5}$ $\frac{11}{6}$

pg. 198

$1\frac{2}{5}$ $3\frac{1}{2}$ $2\frac{1}{3}$

$1\frac{1}{7}$ $4\frac{2}{4}$ $2\frac{2}{6}$

$2\frac{2}{4}$ $7\frac{1}{2}$ $1\frac{3}{8}$

pg. 199

$13\frac{2}{3}$ $13\frac{2}{3}$

$2\frac{6}{8}$ $10\frac{3}{4}$

$5\frac{1}{7}$ $2\frac{1}{8}$

$9\frac{3}{5}$ $1\frac{8}{10}$

$14\frac{3}{4}$ $8\frac{3}{5}$

$4\frac{7}{8}$ $2\frac{5}{10}$

pg. 200

$\frac{3}{10} = .3$

$\frac{7}{10} = .7$

$\frac{8}{10} = .8$

$\frac{9}{10} = .9$

$\frac{5}{10} = .5$

$\frac{6}{10} = .6$

pg. 201

$\frac{12}{100} = .12$ $\frac{36}{100} = .36$

$\frac{28}{100} = .28$ $\frac{50}{100} = .50$

.15 .43 .60
.30 .22 .07
.75 .19 .99

pg. 202

$.01
$.02
$.03
$.05
$.1
$.2
$.25
$.5
$.75
$1.00

pg. 203

.51 .78 .88 .39 .35
.11 .22 5.17 .02 .57
11.29 3.76 12.20 5.62 .34

$.33 $2.12 $.77 $3.53
$8.25 $2.12
$5.99 $.44

pg. 204

.99
.78
.75
.66
.50
.49
.30
.21
.08
.05

pg. 205

$\frac{1}{4} = .25$

$\frac{2}{4} = .5$

$\frac{3}{4} = .75$

$\frac{4}{4} = 1.0$

pg. 206

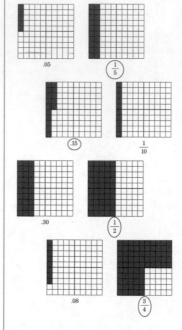

pg. 207

$26.60 $12.00 $19.25 $28.00 $43.44
$7.78 $24.75 $39.80 $32.46 $35.00
$29.28 $60.50 $38.28 $412.50 $217.25
$150 is how much the Seated
Liberty half-dollar is worth today.

pg. 208

$1.43 $1.00 $.13 $7.50 $.21
$1.90 $.84 $.11 $1.81 $.71
$1.43 x 3 = $4.29
$17.49 ÷ 3 = $5.83

pg. 210

F •————————————————• G

A •————————• B

C •——————————————• D

Examples of line segments:

H •————————• I

J •————————————• K

Examples of lines:

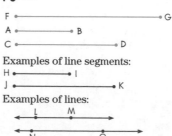

pg. 211

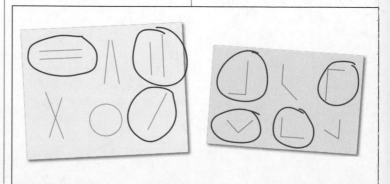

pg. 212

3 4

8 4

6 5

acute right obtuse

pg. 213

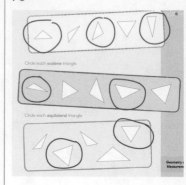

pg. 214

quadrangle hexagon octagon
quadrangle pentagon heptagon
heptagon hexagon quadrangle

pg. 215

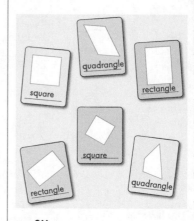

pg. 216

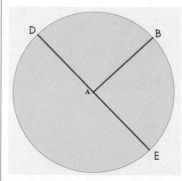

pg. 217
CE   CF   GG   CD
EF
CD
half

pg. 218
1 ½ in.   1 in.
5 in.
7 in.

Pg. 219
9 cm
4 cm   3 cm   2 cm
6 cm   3 cm
4 in   10 cm

pg. 220
12 ft.   66 cm
20 m   28 in.

pg. 221
66 sq. ft.   64 sq. in.
27 sq. m.

pg. 222
24 sq. in.   24 sq. in.   24 sq. in.
yes
yes
yes
yes
6   4   3   8   2   12   1   24
24 sq. in.
yes

pg. 223

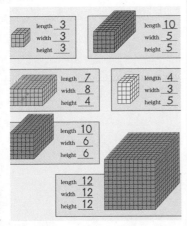

pg. 224
3 x 7 x 2 =   8 x 4 x 2 =
42 cubic in.   64 cubic in.

4 x 4 x 4 =   9 x 6 x 4 =
64 cubic in.   216 cubic in.

pg. 225
2 cups
1 quart
4 oz.
8 cups
1 cup   1 pint   1 quart   1 gallon

pg. 226
80 oz.
3 lbs.
20 lbs., 2 oz.
5,000 lbs.
3 lbs., 9 oz.

pg. 227

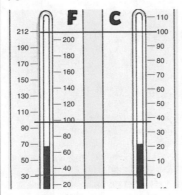

pg. 228
9:13   10:45   12:53
1 hour, 32 minutes
2 hours, 8 minutes
3 hours, 40 minutes

pg. 230
1:6
2:6
3:6

pg. 231
2:16
3:16
1:16
4:16
4:16
2:16

Pg. 232
13:26
13:26
0:26
2:26
1:26

Pg. 233
1:11
2:11
2:11
1:8
1:8
19
2:19
3:19
1:19
B

pg. 234
puppies; parakeets
Jan; June
green
25
Jan
25
Mar
parakeets
June
100; 85

pg. 235
Oct
$31,000
$1,000
$2000; 8
Dec, Jan, April, May
Oct, Mar
May

Pg. 236
months
10
15
more
There were fewer gloves lost.

Pg. 237
Los Robles Elementary School
blue; car
green; bus
bike
3.5%
38%
yes

pg. 240
22   18
ten thousands
                43,262
654,321
                6
$6.23

Pg. 241
30 39 49
$40,105
$21.25   320
399
590,000

Pg. 242
10 < 15   59
$48
49   4,160
no
yes

Pg. 243
16   18,840
4
97 minutes
12   50 minutes
                 48

Pg. 244
4 ounces
$4\frac{2}{3}$
$4.95
.03, .30, 3.03, 3.30
$294.84

Pg. 245
54 minutes
1 hour, 15 minutes
$7\frac{3}{10}$
.2
$2\frac{1}{8}$ cups

Pg. 246
$2\frac{7}{8}$ 2.8
EF
345 354 534 543 435 453
c. a right angle

pg. 247

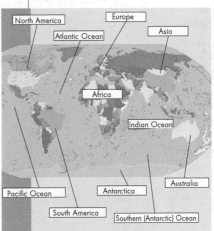

pg. 248
90 sq. ft   8 sq. yards
$10.10
190 ft.
96 cm   1925 sq. cm
68 cups

pg. 250

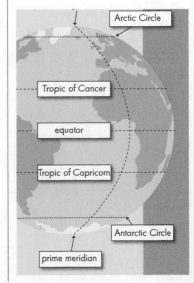

pg. 251
desert
Africa, Asia
tundra or ice
grasslands
South America; North America; Asia
North

pg. 253

pg. 254

Food:

1679 - pressure cooker
1834 - refrigerator
1900 - tractor
1906 - cornflakes

Clothing:

1589 - knitting machine
1891 - zipper

Communication:

1774 - telegraph
1876 - telephone
1884 - fountain pen
1979- cellular phone

pg. 255

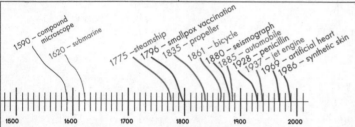

pg. 256

Georgia (GA)
Atlantic Ocean
New York (NY)
Connecticut (CT)
Virginia (VA)

pg. 257

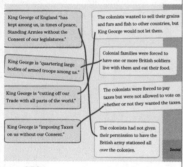

pg. 259

People headed west in search of land or gold.
Missouri
2,000 miles
river crossings; thunderstorms; winter conditions

pg. 260

1790
1890
Georgia
New York; Pennsylvania
Georgia
Massachusetts
1790

pg. 263

Utah; Colorado; Arizona; New Mexico
Hawaii
Maine

pg. 271

• planets; asteroids; comets; satellites; black holes; nebulae; dark matter
• spiral; elliptical; irregular
• the Big Bang theory
• clouds of cosmic dust and gas
• dark matter
• the Milky Way
• cosmos

pg. 272

Neptune
Mercury
Jupiter
Pluto
Mars
Uranus
Earth
Saturn
Venus

pg. 275

new moon
full moon
waxing crescent; waning crescent
half moon
27 days, 7 hours
The word "moon"
waxing gibbous; waning gibbous

pg. 277

7,926 miles in diameter
by studying rocks
the Earth's atmosphere
365.26 days, or one year
24 hours, or one day
93 million miles away

pg. 278

hurricane
flood
earthquake
wind
glacier
volcano

pg. 279

copper
lava
talc
shale
graphite
granite

pg. 280

solid   solid
gas   liquid
liquid   gas

pg. 281

• that energy can neither be created nor destroyed
• its core of matter being converted into energy
• 1905

pg. 282

Г
К
К
К
Р

pg. 283

• motion
• potential
• kinetic; because once it starts moving, it has kinetic energy
• because sound travels on waves
• electricity; magnets; solar or wind energy; sound
• gasoline; compressed coils or springs; a boulder at the top of a hill
• nuclear

pg. 284

bud
          leaf
stem
          root

pg. 285

flower
seeds
fruit
roots
flower

1. It carries nutrients from the roots to the leaves.
2. It supports the plants.
3. It holds the leaves high so it can get sunlight.

pg. 286

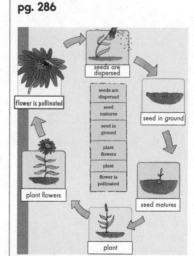

pg. 287

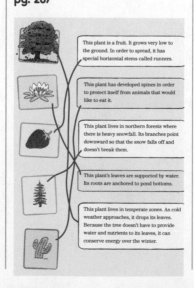

pg. 288

The Food Chain

All living things are linked together by the food chain. Living things that make their own ___food___ are called producers. Plants are producers. They are at the ___bottom___ of the food chain. Animals that eat plants are called ___herbivores___ Animals that eat other animals are called ___carnivores___. Animals that eat both plants and animals are called ___omnivores___. Decomposers such as ___bacteria___ are living things. They break down dead things into very small particles that become part of the ___soil___. Plants need the soil to grow.

pg. 289

D
C
A
F
E
B

pg. 290

          pulley
wedge   axle
          screw

pg. 291

lever
inclined plane

axle   pulley   inclined plane
wedge   lever   screw

pg. 292

unscientific
hypothesis
testing
inside
disproved

pg. 293

air
invisible
prove
scientific
pasteurization

pg. 294

Brain Quest
Extras

Congratulations!

You've finished the Brain Quest Workbook!
In this section, you'll find:

Brain Quest Mini-Deck

Cut out the cards and make your own Brain Quest deck.

Play by yourself or with a friend.

Brainiac Certificate

Put a sticker on each square for every chapter you complete. Finish the whole workbook, and you're an official Brainiac!

And don't forget to turn to the end of the workbook. You'll find stickers and a Map of the Continents!

Questions

Divide 80 cents by 5. How much do you get?

 "The cats paws were dirty." Which word needs an apostrophe?

How do you abbreviate "centimeter"?

 What does the contraction "won't" stand for?

Questions

Kyle is 5 feet 2 inches tall. What's his height in inches?

 Find the proper nouns: "Mount Rushmore is in South Dakota."

Examples of equivalent fractions are: $\frac{2}{4}$, $\frac{4}{8}$, $\frac{6}{12}$, True or false?

 Say these words in alphabetical order: eggplant, yam, beet, tomato.

Questions

If one pound of pasta serves 4 kids, how many ounces of pasta does it take to serve 3 kids?

 Which is the helping verb: b–e–e–n or b–e–a–n?

How much is 56×4?

 What is the plural of "calf"?

Questions

Do pints measure size, weight, or volume?

 "My younger sister is in the pool." What is the complete subject of this sentence?

Estimate the product by rounding the numbers in 29×52 to the nearest ten.

 Which word means the opposite of "smooth": round, rough, rouge?

Answers

62 inches (5 × 12 = 60; 60 + 2 = 62)

 Mount Rushmore, South Dakota

true (They are all equal to $\frac{1}{2}$.)

 beet, eggplant, tomato, yam

Answers

16 cents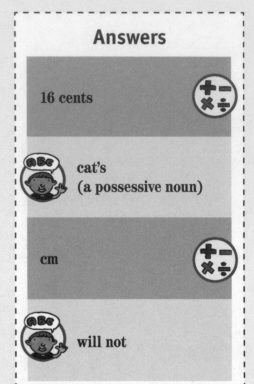

 cat's (a possessive noun)

cm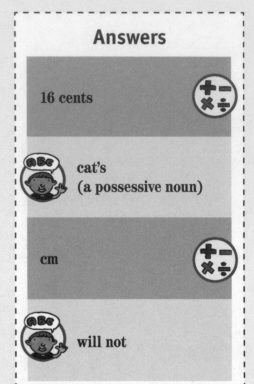

 will not

Answers

volume

 "My younger sister" (All the words in the subject make up the complete subject.)

1,500 (30 × 50)

 rough

Answers

12 ounces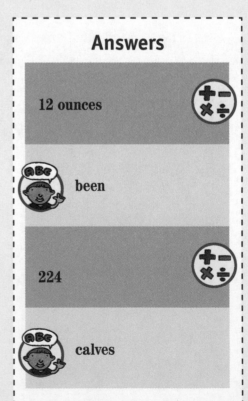

 been

224

 calves

Questions

Subtract 1,563 from 7,394.

What word do you get when you spell "rats" backward?

Which is greater: 8 × 3 or 72 ÷ 6?

Spell the month that follows January.

Questions

Which number is the numerator in the fraction $\frac{6}{15}$?

Which word stays the same in its plural form: cow, sheep, goat?

Subract 62 from 232. Then divide by 5. What's the answer?

How do you abbreviate 231 Waterfront Boulevard?

Questions

Which number is the denominator in the fraction $\frac{12}{48}$?

Which part of "reread" is the prefix?

Which number is a primary number: 4, 7, 9?

Find the adjective in this sentence: "Ann's sweater is very soft."

Questions

Find a synonym of "confuse": surprise, puzzle, alarm.

In the number 231,490, what is the place value of 1?

What is the word for someone who studies stars?

Which is a three-dimensional figure: a triangle or a sphere?

Answers

6

sheep

34

231 Waterfront Blvd.

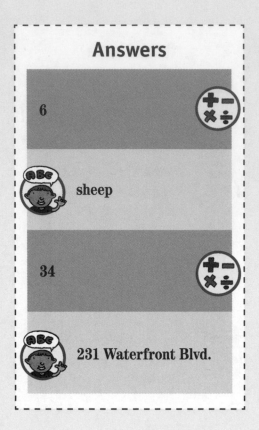

Answers

5,831

star

8 × 3 (24 is greater than 12.)

F–e–b–r–u–a–r–y (February)

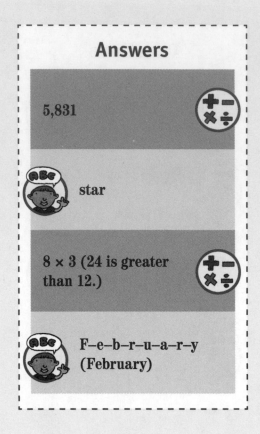

Answers

puzzle

one thousand

astronomer

a sphere

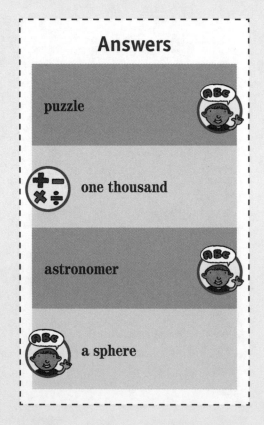

Answers

48

re- (A prefix begins a word.)

7

soft

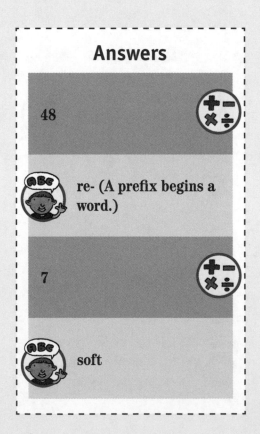

Questions

What is the average of 8, 9, 15, 20?

 Which is correct: "I want that plums" or "I want these plums"?

What is the name of a shape with eight sides?

 What does it mean to be "skating on thin ice"?

Questions

108 divided by 12 equals 9. Which number is the quotient?

 Put the verb in the simple past tense: "Mr. Ramirez teaches us subtraction."

Chitra went to college from 1998 to 2002. How many years was she there?

 Correct this sentence: "I are not hungry."

Questions

Find the equivalent fractions in this group: $\frac{1}{3}, \frac{2}{3}, \frac{2}{6}, \frac{3}{6}$.

 Find the antonym of "perfect": imperfect, unperfect, nonperfect.

How much money is 23¢ × 15?

 Rearrange the letters in the word "earth" to find an internal organ.

Questions

How much is 13 + 15 + 19?

 Which is the first syllable of "marzipan": m–a–r, m–a–r–z–i, or p–a–n?

How many years are in a half-century?

 In recipes, how is the word "teaspoon" abbreviated?

Answers

9

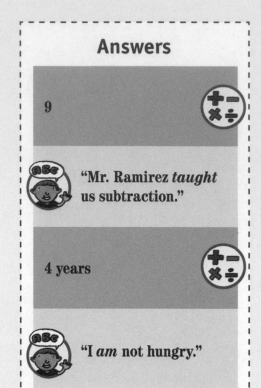

"Mr. Ramirez *taught* us subtraction."

4 years

"I *am* not hungry."

Answers

13

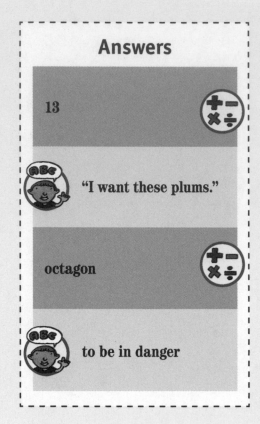

"I want these plums."

octagon

to be in danger

Answers

47

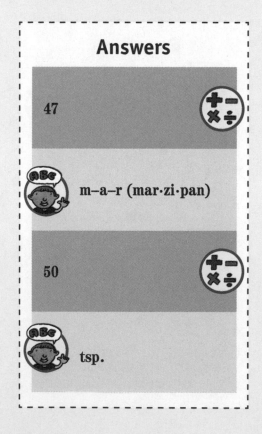

m–a–r (mar·zi·pan)

50

tsp.

Answers

$\frac{1}{3}, \frac{2}{6}$

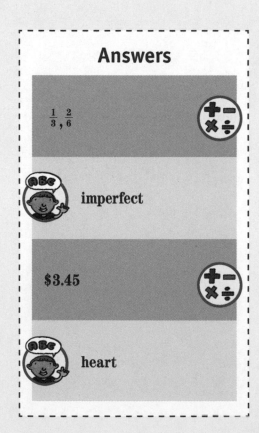

imperfect

$3.45

heart

Questions

What is the average of 2, 4, 6, 8, 10?

 What silent letter do "plumber" and "thumb" have in common?

Find the numbers that are multiples of 3: 6, 13, 16, 24.

 If someone has written a biography, is it fiction or nonfiction?

Questions

Joe has a quarter and 3 pennies. Eva has a dime, a nickel, and 6 pennies. Who has more?

 Which is listed first in the dictionary: "anchor" or "anchovy"?

What is the sum of 4.27 and .83?

 How many syllables are in the word "Mississippi"?

Questions

Which is greater: $\frac{15}{2}$ or $\frac{40}{6}$?

 "Weekends are the funnest days." Find the mistake in this sentence.

The area of the room is 40 square feet. Its width is 8 feet. What is its length?

 Spell the plural of "goose."

Questions

Round the sum of 8.3 and 3.1 to the nearest whole number.

 Find the complete predicate: "Amir and Liam walked to the post office."

Is $\frac{21}{8}$ the same as $2\frac{5}{8}$, $2\frac{1}{2}$, or $2\frac{3}{8}$.

 Which should be written as one word: fire fighter, fire truck, fire hydrant?

Answers

Joe (He has 28¢;
Eva has only 21¢.)

anchor

5.1

four

Answers

6

b

6, 24

nonfiction

Answers

11 (The sum is 11.4.)

walked to the post
office

$2\frac{5}{8}$

firefighter

Answers

$\frac{15}{2}$

funnest
(The superlative
form is "most fun.")

5 feet (40 ÷ 8 = 5)

g–e–e–s–e (geese)

Questions

Which is an improper fraction: $\frac{9}{8}$ or $\frac{7}{8}$?

 If something is tri-colored, how many colors does it have?

The comic book series costs $24.99. You have $16.50. How much more do you need?

 What is the last syllable in the word "whistle"?

Questions

Which is greater: $\frac{2}{3} + \frac{1}{3}$ or $\frac{5}{6} + \frac{1}{6}$?

 Which word is an example of onomatopoeia: smile, growl, laugh, frown?

What time is it if it's 34 minutes after 6:41 P.M.?

 Which is the proper spelling: I–l–l–i–n–o–i–s or I–l–l–i–n–o–y?

Questions

Subtract 26 from 233. Then divide by 9. What do you get?

 Which part of the word "disgraceful" is the suffix?

It snowed 7 days in September. What fraction of the month was snowy?

 Fix this sentence: "Jack go outside and plays with his dog."

Questions

Bryony has one and a half dollars. Ali has 5 quarters and 10 pennies. Who has more?

 What silent letter do these words share: hedge, wedge, ledge?

Is the sum of 22,425 + 6,423 + 150 greater or less than 29,000?

 Complete this analogy: *Portrait* is to *painting* as *novel* is to _____.

Answers

They're the same.

 growl

7:15 P.M.

 I–l–l–i–n–o–i–s

Answers

$\frac{9}{8}$ (because the numerator is bigger than the denominator.)

 three

$8.49 ($24.99 − $16.50 = $8.49)

 tle (whis·tle)

Answers

Bryony ($1.50 is worth more than $1.35.)

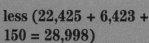 d

less (22,425 + 6,423 + 150 = 28,998)

 *writing*

Answers

23

 ful
(A suffix ends a word.)

$\frac{7}{30}$

 "Jack *goes* outside and plays with his dog."

Questions

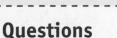 Find the two equivalent fractions in this group: $\frac{2}{2}$, $\frac{3}{9}$, $\frac{5}{12}$, $\frac{6}{18}$.

 What two letters make the sound "f" in the word "enough"?

 If you have 62 nickels, how much do you have in dollars and cents?

 Find the synonym of "forceful": helpful, powerful, dreadful.

Questions

 Add $\frac{5}{7}$ and $\frac{6}{7}$, then give your answer in a mixed number.

 Which country comes first in the dictionary: United States or United Kingdom?

 Our group bought 6 movie tickets. Each cost $8.50. What was the total cost?

 Spell the possessive of "horse."

Questions

 If one train can carry 165 passengers, how many trains would you need to carry 1,320 passengers?

 "Run quickly if you want to catch the bus." Which words are the action verbs?

 Divide 85 by 25. Do you get 3 with a remainder of 20 or 3 with a remainder of 10?

 Which word has three syllables: anagram or enumerate?

Questions

 200° Fahrenheit is warmer than 100° Centigrade. True or false?

 What does it mean if you "get a kick out of" something?

 Find the product of 88 × 33.

 Fix this sentence: "Liz see a snake yesterday."

Answers

$1\frac{4}{7}$ ($\frac{5}{7}$ + $\frac{6}{7}$ = $\frac{11}{7}$ = $1\frac{4}{7}$)

 United Kingdom

$51.00
(6 × $8.50 = $51.00)

 H–o–r–s–e–'–s horse's

Answers

$\frac{3}{9}$, $\frac{6}{18}$

 gh

$3.10 ($.05 × 62)

 powerful

Answers

false (212° Fahrenheit is equal to 100° Centigrade.)

 You enjoy it.

2,904

 "Liz *saw* a snake yesterday."

Answers

8

 run, catch

3 with a remainder of 10

anagram

Brainiac Award!

Every time you finish a chapter of this workbook, choose a Brain Quest sticker and place it over the correct square on the certificate below. When all the squares have been covered by stickers, you will have completed the entire Brain Quest Workbook! Woo-hoo! Congratulations! That's quite an achievement.

Once you have a completed certificate, write your name on the line—or use the alphabet stickers—and cut out the award certificate.

Show your friends. Hang it on your wall! You're a certified Brainiac!

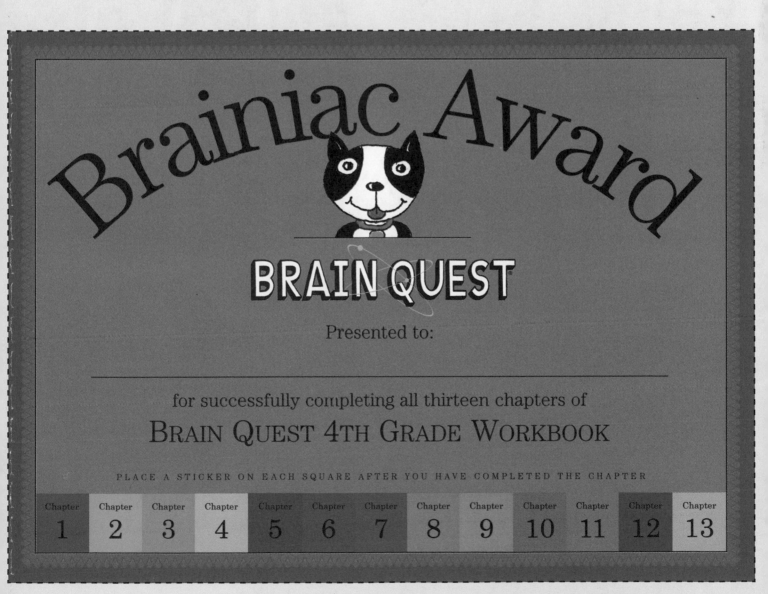

Brainiac Award

BRAIN QUEST

Presented to:

_____

for successfully completing all thirteen chapters of

BRAIN QUEST 4TH GRADE WORKBOOK

PLACE A STICKER ON EACH SQUARE AFTER YOU HAVE COMPLETED THE CHAPTER

| Chapter 1 | Chapter 2 | Chapter 3 | Chapter 4 | Chapter 5 | Chapter 6 | Chapter 7 | Chapter 8 | Chapter 9 | Chapter 10 | Chapter 11 | Chapter 12 | Chapter 13 |